RICHMOND
ITS PEOPLE AND ITS STORY

A SUMMERTIME GLIMPSE OF THE CAPITOL, RICHMOND
(By Courtesy of Richmond Chamber of Commerce.)

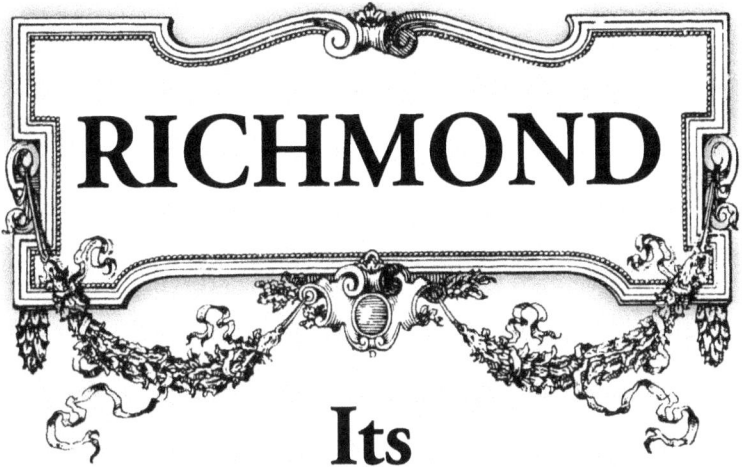

RICHMOND

Its

People

and

Its Story

WITH
83 ILLUSTRATIONS

Mary Newton Stanard

Author of "Colonial Virginia: Its People and Customs," etc.

HERITAGE BOOKS
2016

PREFACE

In planning this book the design of both publisher and author was to set forth the story of Richmond readably told, agreeably printed and sufficiently illustrated, in a single volume of comfortable format. Neither a record of all the facts and dates in Richmond's life of more than three centuries, nor a directory of even its more or less prominent citizens was contemplated. Rather, with due regard to accuracy, the spirit of the old-young city, its atmosphere and its personality were to be sought and, if possible, imprisoned in the pages of a brief narrative.

The quest has led the party of the first part—meaning myself—to many and varied sources of information, including Captain John Smith's quaint *Historie of Virginia*, and other histories; biographies; public records, letters, diaries, files of newspapers—from the ancient *Virginia Gazette* to those of recent date—and periodicals, early and late, beginning with the *Southern Literary Messenger*.

Of course my husband, William G. Stanard, LL.D., now, and for the past quarter of a century, Secretary of the Virginia Historical Society and Editor of its magazine, has been my companion on this quest and, in addition to the facilities of the Society, and of the Virginia State Library and of our own library, his expert knowledge of *Virginiana* and intelligent and frank criticism of my work have been at my disposal.

To the friends who have aided in securing illustrations I give my hearty thanks. Of these illustrations more than half have never appeared in any other book, and use of many has been for the first time granted especially for this volume.

PREFACE

Readers from a distance who would like to know Richmond better are cordially invited to come in spring with the pansies and irises, when bees are swinging in linden blossoms, or in early summer when roses are embowering porches, or later, when blooms like the lucious hearts of ripe watermelons glow in crêpe-myrtle boughs, or in autumn when maples are ablaze in streets and in parks. At any of these seasons long sections of many streets will be shady green arbors. You will be equally welcome if you come in winter, but do not be surprised if a cold wave has, for a day or perhaps a week, tucked this city which the sun loves into a blanket of snow and fringed it with icicles.

I wish that it had been possible to name the rebuilders of Richmond—those suvivors of the struggle of 1861-65 and their descendants of the generation following, who bound up the wounds of the bruised and broken city and restored it to its first estate, and more. But names that belong in this honor roll are proclaimed in every column of newspapers whose bound files will always be easily accessible, and current papers have fallen into a pleasant habit of having these files searched and, daily in their news of old Richmond, reminding us of some of the men and women referred to.

A word about the section devoted to the War Between the States.

Of making books and magazine articles considering the Capital of the Confederacy from one or more angles there has been no end. Its political and military history has, of course, filled volumes. Vivid pictures of its home, hospital and social life (many of which have served me as sources) have been drawn. But if there has hitherto been any attempt to convey an impression (sketchily and

PREFACE

untechnically, of course) upon a single canvas, of the whole kaleidoscopic scene—military, public, economic, home, hospital, social, literary, even the current jokes— with white persons and negroes, grown persons and children, rich and poor, high and low in their relations to the place and one another, I do not know of it.

It has seemed unsuitable to burden with notes the pages of a work of this kind, but every statement made is based on good authority.

MARY NEWTON STANARD

RICHMOND, VIRGINIA

CONTENTS

CONTENTS

PART VI
THE WAR BETWEEN THE STATES, AND RECONSTRUCTION
(1859–1870)

ILLUSTRATIONS

ILLUSTRATIONS

ILLUSTRATIONS

PROLOGUE

THE GREY CROSS ON THE HILL

Now and then in the City of Richmond, in Virginia, as in other places these latter days, are heard hummings and whirrings such as never reached the ear of earlier generations. People look up to see some inquisitive Bird-man hovering overhead, circling, and dipping as he seeks a nearer view of the reds and yellows and greys of roofs and buildings crowding one another sociably up hill and down dale on both sides of a winding river. The air in which the Bird-man moves is pierced by church spires and towering buildings, and by smoke-stacks of factories throwing off bannerlike, grey veils through which he makes out a criss-cross of streets. Some of these are lined with ample homes and fringed with trees; a few of them adorned with statuary. Others have rows of toy-village houses. Others still are streams of rushing traffic between currents of slower-moving human life, walled in by temples of commerce.

As he swoops lower the Bird-man may make out busy market-places and a few squalid spots, like sores, from which he will look quickly away to quiet, green parks agleam with still lakelets and splotches of color which perhaps are the blooms of bedded plants, perhaps the dresses of children, playing.

Lower, and lower still he dips his wings and hears the tumult and shouting of progress and the laughter of prosperity, and he fancies that he catches an undertone which may be the weeping of those in sorrow or the groans of those in pain.

PROLOGUE

As the Bird-man looks and listens the spirit of Prophecy may, all unseen, seat herself beside him and begin to show him some of the wonders of the future, but Memory leans over his shoulder and whispers that if he would see this city in true perspective he must alight and seek out the background from which she has fashioned the setting which gives it not merely a location, a name and structures of brick and stone and steel, but personality and atmosphere peculiarly its own.

So, choosing a bold hilltop whose velvet terraces rise out of the very midst of traffic and trade and manufacture, he makes a landing and gazes at closer range upon the picture spreading around him. He finds that he is standing in the shadow of a granite cross whose base is a mound of rough stones (evidently gathered from the river) held together by cement. Upon the Grey Cross are written these words:

Capt. Christopher Newport   John Smith
Gabriel Archer   Hon George Percy
With Gentlemen, Marines, Soldiers, To The Number Of Twenty-One, Explored James River To The Falls And Set Up A Cross Whitsunday, June 10th, 1607.

This Monument Is Presented To The City of Richmond By The Association For The Preservation of Virginia Antiquities.
June 10th, 1907.

"Dei Gratia Virginia Condita."

As the Bird-man reads he perceives that, though Prophecy has deserted him, Memory is still with him. She points to the river below, where, on a green islet he seems to see another cross, hastily constructed of rough pieces of wood bearing the legend "Jacobus Rex 1607", and to hear the exulting shout of a band of Englishmen in the

THE GREY CROSS ON THE HILL

LIBBY HILL, THE CONFEDERATE SOLDIERS' AND SAILORS' MONUMENT, AND JAMES RIVER.

CAPTAIN JOHN SMITH
The bronze statue at Jamestown

curling locks, rakish hats and doublets and hose of that long past day, who erected it. As if by magic, terraced Gamble's Hill has become a rugged and wooded promontory in a wilderness standing out above a river flowing boisterously down from between other wooded hills, creating a series of little waterfalls as it races over a stony bed and becomes navigable. The only signs of human life are the quaintly clad, sunburned men, grouped about the rude cross on the islet and some naked, gyrating Indians staring at them; the only signs of human habitation the dozen or so huts of a palisaded Indian village further down the river.

The scene changes. Memory shows him a group more than a century later, whose leader, viewing this same land —then dotted with cultivated clearings scattered with homesteads—and noting a resemblance to the site of Richmond on the Thames, tosses off a toast and jocundly projects not a castle only, but a city in the air, by that token unconsciously dubbing himself for future generations, the Father of Richmond on the James.

The Bird-man lays aside his field glasses, which have become rather a hindrance than a help, and accepts those proffered by Memory with which he can see not only through smoke-screens of busy factories, but through view-obstructing buildings and can recognize quaintness peeping with fascinating unexpectedness over the shoulders of newness. He sees beyond the sky-scrapers that come between a tiny white church, on a distant hill, from one of whose pews rang the slogan " Give me liberty or give me death!" Halfway between the white church and the Grey Cross (on still another green hill) he sees the pillared porticoes of the Capitol of Virginia and of the Confederacy. At a little distance to the south and west he makes out a dingy office-building and a face in a window—the

white, care-lined face of a poet whom disaster followed
—bending over a desk, setting down deathless words. Not
far away he picks out The Old Stone House of many traditions, and at a little distance to the north and west, a
pile of mellow red brick—the simple, sturdy homestead of
America's most renowned Chief Justice. He gazes dream-
ily on the sign of the Swan Tavern, where the poet and the
Chief Justice and many others of earlier day took their
ease; on the house in which Thackeray was a guest when
he found Richmond "the merriest town in America";
on the one in which "Mr. Charles Dickens and Lady" were
lodged and on the theatre where charming Joe Jefferson
played "Rip Van Winkle" and many other rôles. In
dusty old streets he detects footprints of Washington and
Lafayette, of Monroe and Madison and of Lee. Through
dim windows of dilapidated houses he sees the light of
many candles streaming from a gala-night illumination.
Doors, of houses no longer existing, open wide to admit
gaily attired guests, to welcome the affianced lover of a
reigning belle, or to speed the parting of a distinguished
but rejected suitor.

With Memory as guide, old paving-stones tell stories,
old trees gossip, old streets become picture-books, old
houses store-houses of strange lore.

As the story of Richmond began with the wooden cross
of Whitsunday 1607, the commemorative Grey Cross on
the hill erected exactly three hundred years later, has
seemed a natural place at which to begin this book.

PART I
THE COLONIAL PERIOD
(1607—1774)

RICHMOND
ITS PEOPLE AND ITS STORY

CHAPTER I

STRUGGLES WITH THE INDIANS

VIRGINIA in 1607 was a new Eden and its story of conquest of the earth and carving out of homes is the record of a new beginning of the white race in a new world.

The history of Richmond began just four weeks after the arrival of Englishmen at Jamestown.

Its first chapter is made up of struggles with the Indians for a foothold for white men at " The Falls " of that waterway which the red men had named for their king, " The River Powhatan ", but the English promptly rechristened for theirs, " King James His River "—or " James River."

It was a struggle for a safe spot where the new-comer might make a clearing and build him a house of logs from the woods, chinked with mud, or of stones gathered from the river-bed or blasted out of the ground, and chinked with mortar; a safe spot to which to bring an English maiden who would transform the cabin or the cottage into a home about which the new Adam and Eve would plant a garden; a safe spot where children could be born and reared close to nature's heart and in which the wife could be left with her babies and housewifery while the husband went forth to till the fields or to fish and hunt in river and forest for food to serve in wooden trenchers or pewter platters, on the table sawed from a felled oak or brought over on a late ship from " home."

When, on Sunday, June 10, 1607, white men looked for the first time on what was to be this spot, they looked with mingled " content and grief ", for though they were charmed with the islet-dotted river and its green, flower-besprinkled banks, the hunter's paradise beyond beckoned them to further exploration; but the river shouted from its rocky bed to the " shallop " in which they had sailed from Jamestown: " Thus far and no further!"

As the commemorative Grey Cross shows, they were a party of gentlemen and sailors under the doughty admiral Christopher Newport, who had conducted the three little ships, *Susan Constant, Godspeed* and *Discovery* from England to Virginia. Among them were at least three whose goose-quills were pens of ready writers—Captain John Smith, Master George Percy and Master Gabriel Archer—and all three used them during this trip. Master Archer, glancing about him with unconsciously prophetic eye, scribbled in his note-book—and the earliest dim dream of busy Richmond on the James had become a matter of record. This is what he wrote:

" Here the water falls Downe through great mayne Rockes from ledges of Rockes above....in which fall it maketh Divers little Isletts, on which might be placed 100 water milnes for any uses."

The country in the neighborhood was in possession of Indians under Little Powhatan—a chief who was subordinate to *Great* Powhatan.

The squaws and braves, full of interest in the novelty of men with white, bearded faces and clothed bodies, entertained them with dancing at various points along the river, brought them wheat, beans, mulberries, straw-berries, and " baskets full of dried oysters ", (for which they bargained tactfully) and gave them a guide who " proved a very trustye frend." On the day after their

4

MEN'S DRESS AT ABOUT THE TIME OF THE WHITE MAN'S FIRST VISIT TO
PRESENT SITE OF RICHMOND, 1607

GENTLEMEN'S DRESS AT THE TIME OF BACON'S REBELLION, 1676

HOW RICHMONDERS DRESSED IN 1745

A DUCKING STOOL

arrival at The Falls they entertained Little Powhatan at the first diplomatic dinner of record in America. The Indian "ate very freshly" of their meat, drank of their beer, aqua vitæ and sack, and in dramatic pantomime they made him understand that his friends were their friends, his enemies their enemies. After the feast they had a friendly chat with him (in sign language, of course) "sitting upon the bank by the overfall, beholding the same." He discouraged their proceeding further overland—making them understand that they "should get no victuals and be tired", and that the chief of the country higher up was his enemy "that came downe at the fall of the leafe and invaded his countreye."

"Captain Newport . . . decided to explore no further for the present. . . . So upon one of the little Isletts at the mouth of the falls" (runs the Archer record), "he sett up a Crosse with this inscription, Jacobus Rex 1607, and his own name belowe. At the erecting thereof we prayed for our king and our owne prosperous success in this his Actyon and proclaymed him kyng, with a great showte."

Thus was staked the white man's claim to the red man's country—the cross representing the Church of England and the name of King James, in solemn Latin, the Crown. Naviraus, the guide, "began to admire", but "our Captayne told him that the two armes of the Crosse signifyed King Powhatah and himselfe, the fastening of it in the myddest was their united Leag, and the shoute the reverence he dyd to Powhatah, which cheered Naviraus not a little", says Master Archer.

That night Little Powhatan would have returned their entertainment, but said that their "hot drinks" had caused him "grief", so they excused him, presented him with a hatchet and gave him "the kindest farewell that possibly might be." By morning the Indian had sufficiently recovered from his first spree to have a deer roasted in their honor and red men and white " satt banquetting all the forenoon."

Thus was sealed the first American League of Nations.

There is a slight suggestion of the manner of the Four Evangelists in the writing of the three recorders of the beginning of Richmond's story, in the way each sets down faithfully the events as he saw them, verifying one another by the differences as well as the likenesses of the testimony. Percy's observations show the poetic fancy and diction characteristic of this son of an Earl of Northumberland. " When wee had finished and set up our Crosse ", he writes, " we shipt our men and made for James Fort . . This river is one of the famousest rivers that ever was found by any Christian . . . Wheresoever we landed . . . wee saw the goodliest woods . . . and all the grounds bespred with many sweet and delicate flowers . . .There are also many fruites, as Strawberries, Mulberries, Raspberries, and Fruites unknown."

Captain Smith is explicit and graphic: " The people in all places kindly intreating us, daunsing and feasting us with Strawberries, Mulberries, Bread, Fish and other of their countrie provisions . . . for which Captaine Newport kindly requited their least favours with Bels, Pinnes, Needles, beades [looking] Glasses, which so contented them that his liberalitie made them follow us from place to place, and ever kindly respect us . . . Whitsunday, after dinner . . . we erected a Cross."

The staking of the white man's claim at The Falls was a picturesque incident of a June Sunday, but he was to find that the land which, little by little, he made his own had to be defended by forts and by the spending of powder and shot, the spilling of blood, through nearly a hundred years before there was such thing as lying down in safety in homes on the ground now covered by the city of Richmond.

In the fall of 1609 John Ratcliffe, then President of the Virginia Council, wrote to the Prime Minister of England: "We have planted 100 men at The Falls." Earlier that year Captain Francis West, brother of Lord Delaware, had been sent with 120 men to make a settlement there, which he named—for himself—West Fort. But James River, on one of the rampages to which heavy rains made it subject, forced them to the higher ground of " Fort Powhatan," which Captain Smith bought from the Indians but rechristened None Such, because there was " no place so strong, so pleasant and delightful in Virginia." Here they were " seated gallantlie", but when the river rested contentedly within its banks again they went back to West Fort, nearer their boats. Soon afterward they abandoned the attempted settlement altogether, and returned to Jamestown.

Two years later a town called Henrico, for Prince Henry, was begun at the present Dutch Gap, fourteen miles below The Falls, and in 1619 the earliest iron works in America were established at Falling Creek (only six miles below The Falls), and the eight miles of land between The Falls and Henrico was granted for a college and university for English and Indian youths. This land was to be rented out and cultivated to raise an endowment fund. Plans for the college were going ahead briskly when the ghastly Indian massacre of 1622 put an end to both it and the iron works.

As late as 1639 the highest settled point on the river was four or five miles below The Falls and was given the name of World's End. In 1644 the Assembly in session at Jamestown ordered the erection at The Falls of a fort, for defense against the Indians, to be called Fort Charles.

On the north bank of the river seven hills waited for Richmond to come and spread her skirts over them, on the south bank (the site of the town of Manchester, whose earliest name was Rocky Ridge, and whose latest, South Richmond), fertile low-grounds waited for the plough-share. Two years after the erection of the fort on the north bank the Assembly directed that as there was "no plantable land" adjoining Fort Charles and therefore no encouragement for anybody to maintain the same, any person or persons who would purchase the right of Captain Thomas Harris and seat on the south side of the river opposite the fort should "enjoy the houseing belonging to the said Fort for the use of timber or by burning them for the nails or otherwise, as also shall be exempted from the publique taxes for the term of three yeares, provided that the number exceed not tenn, and also shall have and enjoy the boats and ammunition belonging to said Fort."

For ten years the settlers at The Falls seem to have enjoyed a sufficiently peaceful season to enable them to cease making history and make crops. Then, in 1656, some seven hundred Indians, then called Ricahecrians, now known to have been Senecas from the northwestern part of the present New York, made their way to Virginia and squatted upon the lands at The Falls. Panic followed, for Indians of this tribe were extremely savage and were enemies of the tribes with which the English were then at peace.

Forces under Colonel Edward Hill, of "Shirley" were sent to remove them "without making warr if it may be, only in case of their own defense", and the Indian allies of the English were invited "to treat with the common enemy 'as they see fit'."

Colonel Hill's men, with a hundred Pamunkeys under their chief the "mighty Totopotomoi" were defeated in a

8

battle which gave the name of Bloody Run to a stream (at present concealed by a culvert) near Chimborazo Park, in what is now the city of Richmond.

The next year the Assembly enacted that as Henrico County (of which Richmond is the county seat) was, as a frontier, the part of Virginia most exposed to dangers from the Indians, the bounds within which Indians were allowed to come on the south side of the river be confirmed, and that county militia lay out bounds on the north side. After bounds were laid out and notice given it should be lawful for any Englishman to kill any Indian who should presume to come in, contrary to the Act in force.

CHAPTER II

ENTER THE BYRDS

AMONG gentlemen struggling to plant a settlement at The Falls was Colonel Thomas Stegg, a rich merchant and owner of trading ships, a Councillor, sometime Auditor General, and an intimate friend of the Governor, Sir William Berkeley. He owned lands at The Falls (and slaves to cultivate them) on both sides of the river. He made his home on the south side, in a stone house (with a great stone chimney in the middle), a rough drawing of which may be seen today, on a plat in the *Byrd Title Book*.

And this brings us to the entrance on the American scene of a family which was to play star parts in Virginia's and Richmond's drama for a hundred years. Colonel Stegg died in 1671 leaving his Virginia estate to his nephew William Byrd, a nineteen year old youth of good birth and breeding, of high character and full of energy of mind and body. His portrait, painted in England, shows a beautiful and masterful looking boy of seven or eight years. When he became Colonel Stegg's heir he was already living in Virginia, presumably in his uncle's home at The Falls. It was doubtless to this home that, upon his coming of age, in 1673, he took a twenty year old bride—Mary, the daughter of Colonel Warham Horsmanden, one of the Cavalier refugees to Virginia—who gave up what diversions Jamestown could offer to share with her mate the dangers and loneliness of frontier life.

As time went on, William Byrd—already an extensive planter—was to become a famous Indian trader and

COLONEL WILLIAM BYRD, II, OF "WESTOVER", THE FOUNDER OF RICHMOND
From the portrait at "Brandon"

THE EARLIEST MAP OF RICHMOND

Made by William Mayo for Colonel William Byrd in 1737. Lots 97 and 98, marked "The Church", were given by Colonel Byrd for St. John's, at Grace and Twenty-fifth Streets

A TICKET IN THE BYRD LOTTERY

merchant. His caravans of woodsmen and traders with
as many as a hundred pack-horses laden with English
goods to be exchanged with the natives for furs, were
to be seen filing along a Trading Path which extended more
than four hundred miles into the wilderness—a Trading
Path on which scenes were sometimes enacted which, when
talked over around the campfires at night, made the blood
run cold; for the natives encountered were not always
satisfied with conventional bargain and trade, and the
trophies they displayed were not won at the cost of lives
of wild beasts only. Young Captain Byrd sometimes personally conducted his caravans, and rumors of him and
his exploits and possessions were carried by Indians as far
west as the Mississippi and north as far as Canada.

At The Falls his business embraced importing and
exporting, as well as general merchandise of the most
general description. From England came everything a
rural community might need, from goods to be sold by the
yard and pills by the box, to white servants—to be bound
out for a term of years—including carpenters, bricklayers
and masons, who brought " extraordinary prices." From
Barbadoes came white sugar, rum and molasses. Also,
negro slaves came thence as well as from Africa.

Meantime Mary Byrd was providing the nest at The
Falls with five little Byrds, the first of whom " Will ", was
to become not only the founder of Richmond, but by reason
of his brilliant talents, his culture, his princely appearance
and captivating personality, was to receive the soubriquet
of " The Black Swan of Virginia." A very lucky star with
a particularly merry twinkle must have stood over the
stone house, at the faraway Falls of James River on his
birthnight. When Will was two years old such peace as
his mother could find in that danger-haunted home was
roughly broken by the uprising known as Bacon's Rebel-

11

lion. A month earlier Indian depredations had caused an order that " fifty men out of James City County be garrisoned near The Falls of James River at Captain Byrd's or at one fort or place of defense over against him at Howletts "—in the present South Richmond. Nathaniel Bacon and his wife made their home at Curles Neck, some twelve miles down the river, but had also a plantation, " Bacon's Quarter " (adjoining the Byrd property at The Falls), part of which is now covered by the northwestern section of Richmond. It was the murder by Indians of his overseer there which made him yield to the call, " A Bacon! A Bacon! A Bacon! " from the panic stricken people and lead the militia " commission or no commission " against the red men. It is interesting to remember that his love for his wife, Elizabeth, daughter of Sir Edward Duke, had been of the kind that laughs at locksmiths and that he had borne her away from her father's home, Benhill Lodge, in England, in young Lochinvar fashion—permission or no permission—and notwithstanding the fact that his own father, Thomas Bacon, of Friston Hall, also opposed the match.

Captain Byrd happened to be discussing " the seriousness of the times " with " Squire Bacon " and some other planters at Jordan's Point, when the new Indian depredations, combined with the Governor's indifference to them, brought matters to a head. Byrd at once joined Bacon and led some of his forces from The Falls " a great way south—" into North Carolina, indeed. Before going he placed his wife and little son with friends in the safer regions down the river. Elizabeth Bacon, clutching her baby daughter to her breast, remained in her own home where the enraged Governor Berkeley in his fruitless pursuit of " General Bacon by consent of the people", stopped long enough to inform her that her husband would hang as soon as he came back. Each of these young wives of planters of the frontier settlement which was to become Richmond, wrote a graphic letter home describing the Rebellion.

Three times during the Rebellion the neighborhood of The Falls rang with Nathaniel Bacon's eloquence as he made his "hearts of gold" (as he called his men) the brief but thrilling speeches with which he urged them on. So suggestive in spirit and in phrase are these speeches of those of Patrick Henry, that one wonders if their echo could have been held in the air, too fine for human ear, and communicated to the brain of the patriot of a hundred years later.

In less than a year all was quiet, Bacon dead and the pretty picture his wife made, with her baby in her arms, lost to the neighborhood. But disastrous as was the ending of the Rebellion one of its several happy results was comparative safety from the Red Peril for Eastern Virginia. In the following year—1677—the Indian tribes of that section made a treaty of peace with the Colonists, after which presents and insignia of authority were sent from England to various Chiefs. The Queen of Pamunkey received a red velvet cap with a suitably inscribed silver frontlet, which is now in the collection of the Association for the Preservation of Virginia Antiquities, at the John Marshall House, in Richmond.

Precautions were still necessary, however. In the summer of 1678 a party of Indians came down from the northward to The Falls, attacking white people and red people alike. The county militia was sent against them and drove them off, but the commanding officers, Colonel Francis Eppes and Major William Harris, were killed. In the following April the Assembly ordered that " on the south side of James River above Captain Byrd's be established one stone house or garrison, with a small house for ammunition." In the same month Byrd was granted a tract five miles long on both sides of the river one mile "backwards in the woods on the south side, and two miles on the north side, who agreed to seat and have in readiness upon all occasions on beate of drumm, fifty able men, well armed, with sufficient ammunition and provisions for the country service in defense of the inhabitants against the enemy Indian." This grant was not confirmed in England, but much of the land was already Byrd's by inheritance, and he gradually acquired the rest.

Though now in safety from Indians the Byrds were to find an enemy as subtle in the river. The story of Richmond is punctuated with the word freshet as the Psalms of David are with Selah. At intervals from the beginning all other activities have paused to deal with the ambitious river which has risen out of its bounds to destroy much property and some lives. The great freshet of 1771 which devastated the land, swept vessels from their moorings and carried away houses, trees and mills, is a matter of history. In the words of an eye witness: "Many islands have been torn to pieces, hills of sand thrown up, channels stopt and their courses altered and, in short, the Face of Nature almost changed." Persons still living in Richmond have seen boats on lower Main Street and women and children rescued from windows of houses standing in water. Most of the streets have now been elevated above danger line, so that the river is no longer a serious menace.

In a letter to "Father Horsmanden" in England, dated June 5, 1685, Colonel Byrd wrote: "About five weeks since here happened such a deluge that the like hath not been heard of in the memory of man; the water overflowing all my plantation came into my dwelling house. It

14

swept away all our fences, destroyed all that was on the ground and carryed away the Hills (that were made for tobacco) with all the top of the manured land, and what's more strange, carryed a mill (stones, House and all, as they were standing) about 150 yards down the Creek. . . The water hath ruined my crop and most of my neighbors', so that we shall make little this year."

As the Byrd youngsters grew they were sent over seas to be properly polished. Letters show that at the ages of nine and six, Will and Susan were at boarding school there in 1683, and in 1685, urged by his wife, Colonel Byrd sent four-year-old Ursula, pet-named " Little Nutty ", over to the Horsmandens. He wrote a letter to each of his brothers and sisters—six letters in all—commending the baby to their love and care. Giving her up was hard, but she must have a chance to become a lady and in one of these letters he says : " I must confesse she could learn nothing good in a great family of negroes." On the same day he wrote Will :

" Dear Son, I received your letter and am glad to hear you are with so good a master who I hope will see you improve your time and that you bee carefull to serve God as you ought, without which you cannot expect to doe well here or hereafter."

In charge of a maid, " Little Nutty " was sent in a toy ship over endless deep waters to another world, and it is not likely that she ever saw The Falls or her pickaninny playmates again. Before she was out of Hackney boarding school, near London, her parents were established at their new home, " Westover ", and it was to a house earlier than the present mansion, on that plantation, that she afterward returned. Before her seventeenth birthday she had been married to Robert Beverley, the Virginia historian, and lay under a stone in Jamestown churchyard, leaving a son, William, who built "Blandfield", the ancestral home of many of the Beverleys. Her name, "Little Nutty", taken in connection with the portrait of her brother Will and other portraits of the Byrd family, make it easy to see, in fancy, this earliest little maid of The Falls of James River of whom anything is known— eyes dark and flashing under black brows and lashes, ringlets brown like the nuts in the woods, mouth a wild strawberry from the fields.

CHAPTER III

THE BEGINNING OF RICHMOND TOWN

AFTER the removal of Colonel Byrd to " Westover ", he continued to conduct his business at The Falls through agents and overseers and was often there himself, and on the land where the white man's claim had been staked with a cross, the struggling settlement gradually grew and spread. England was to make of his son William an accomplished scholar, a finished courtier, a versatile man of the world, but was not to destroy his love of the woods and of expanses of earth, and water and sky imbibed with his mother's milk and kept alive in his days of paddling —like Richmond boys of later generations—in frothy water at The Falls, playing hide and seek in groves filled with bird-music and listening to hunters' tales of adventure with Indians, bears and wolves.

And so, after a lapse of years in which William Byrd I made his exit from Virginia and the world, young Will, now known as Colonel William Byrd II, came home, took up life at " Westover " where he built the present house, was twice married and became the father of still another Will and several daughters who grew up to be belles and heroines of romance. From " Westover " he wrote to a friend in England : " A Library, a Garden, a Grove and a Purling stream are the innocent scenes that divert our Leisure." To quote him again, however, he " detested idleness ", and it is usually in some form of activity that we find him. Happily, he kept diaries which preserve for all time a style of writing which critics agree has been equalled in vigor and charm by no American of the Colonial period save Franklin.

When, after the half-century which has passed since the nine-year-old boy's departure for England the curtain rises once more on The Falls, we find the man of nine-and-fifty, fit as a fiddle, occupying the centre of the stage and viewing from his saddle the land of his earliest memories, many, many acres of which are now his own. It is September of the year 1733 and he is on a " Journey " to his tract, "The Land of Eden", in North Carolina. With him are Major William Mayo, who goes as Surveyor, Major James Munford, Mr. John Banister, Mr. Peter Jones, five woodsmen, four negroes and three Indians. In his diary of this " Journey " Colonel Byrd says: " When we got home we laid the foundation of two large Citys. One. . . to be called Richmond, and the other . . .to be nam'd Petersburgh. These Major Mayo offered to lay out into Lots without Fee or Reward. The Truth of it is, these two places being the uppermost Landing of James and Appamattux Rivers, are naturally intended for Marts, where the Traffick of the Outer Inhabitants must Center. Thus we did build not Castles only, but also Citys in the Air."

In lively words he paints the experiences of his party and the cheerfulness with which they accepted whatever Fortune sent—unconsciously giving the reader a picture of the man who was to be the Father of Richmond. For instance:

" The Water was risen so high that it ran into the Top of my Boots, but without giving me any cold, altho I rid in my wet stockings."

" My greatest disaster was that in mounting one of the precipices, my steed made a Short turn and gave my knee an unmerciful Bang against a tree, and I felt the effects of it several Days after. However, this was no Interruption of our Journey, but we went merrily on."

ST. JOHN'S CHURCH

THE ISLETS OF JAMES RIVER OPPOSITE RICHMOND

THE BEGINNING OF RICHMOND TOWN

" I Hurt my other Knee this afternoon, but not, enough to spoil either my dancing or my Stomach."

" We took up our Quarters at the same Camp where we had a little before been alarmed with the Supposed Indian Whistle, which we could hardly get out of our heads. However, it did not Spoil our rest; but we dreamt all Night of the delights of Tempe and the Elysian Fields."

In the diary of an earlier expedition (to run the Dividing Line between Virginia and North Carolina) he says:

" Our Landlord had a tolerable good House and Clean Furniture, and yet we could not be tempted to lodge in it. We chose rather to lye in the open Field, for fear of growing too tender. A clear sky, spangled with Stars was our Canopy, which being the last thing we saw before we fell asleep, gave us magnificent Dreams. The Truth of it is, we took so much pleasure in that natural kind of Lodging, that I think at the foot of the Account Mankind are great Losers by the Luxury of Feather Beds and warm apartments."

His readiness to take everything as it came reached its peak when he wrote: " In our way we killed two very large Rattle Snakes . . . but nobody would be persuaded to carry them to our Quarters, altho they would have added much to the Luxury of our Supper."

To prove that rattlesnake had never been the chief of his diet and resuscitate any gentle reader for whom the shock of this last entry may have been disastrous, the favorite recipe of his father for cooking " ye ham in perfection " is given here. The first Colonel Byrd preserved this recipe by writing it down where it was most certain to be safe for his own use and for posterity—on a fly-leaf of his Bible: " To eat ye Ham in Perfection steep it in Half Milk and half Water for Thirty-six hours, and then having brought the water to a Boil put ye Ham therein and let it simmer, not boil, for 4 or 5 Hours according to size of ye Ham—for simmering brings ye Salt out and boiling drives it in."

In April of the year 1737—three years and a half after two cities in the air had been thus merrily planned—the one that was to be named Richmond was given a foundation on solid ground, when Major Mayo redeemed his promise and laid out a little checkerboard of thirty-two squares, each of which contained four lots. The principal streets were named for letters of the alphabet, the cross streets for numerals. The lower or southern edge of the checkerboard, four squares long and eight wide, rested on D Street, along the river front—now Cary Street; the upper edge on the present Broad Street. Its western edge ran along what was then First but is now Seventeenth Street, and its eastern tilted up to the brow of what was then known as Richmond Hill, but later, as other heights were taken into the town limits, was called Church Hill on account of St. John's—for which Colonel Byrd gave two lots in the northeast corner of the checkerboard, on the hill-top, " with any pine timber they can find on that side of Shockoe Creek and wood for burning brick into the bargain."

In the high land north and east of the checkerboard Major Mayo's map shows twelve lots, varying in size from five to seventeen acres, evidently intended for suburban villas with grounds and gardens. Names of these home-sites, such as " Abbington ", " Inglesby ", " Hampstead ", and so on, appear on the map, and on six of them names of men who had already become their owners appear. Streets and houses of later Richmond have long since spread themselves over these estates, but the name of at least one of their owners, Daniel Weisiger, who called his place " Frankfort ", and who is mentioned as a " high

German " in the Henrico County records, remains in Richmond and its neighborhood today. Among the scattered houses as old, or older than the checkerboard, at least two remain. One of them was the home of John Coles a prosperous merchant who had in April 1741 " a cargo of wheat valued at £1500 sterling ready to ship for England ", and whose sons became wealthy planters and left stately homes in Albemarle and Pittsylvania Counties. His house later became the home of Colonel Richard Adams, the most prominent citizen of Richmond in the years immediately preceding the Revolution. It was for him, and not for an Adams of national distinction, that the street next in order to the present Jefferson Street, was named. His interesting old dormer-windowed house is now a part of Monte Maria Convent, on Church Hill. The initials I. R. which, in early script, appear upon the Old Stone House on lower Main Street, seem to stand for Jacobus Rex. If they do, this fascinating little building about which traditions as tenacious as old ivy have grown and clung, and which, since it became the Edgar Allan Poe Shrine, has taken a new lease on the interest of Richmond and the world at large, must date from the reign of James II, which ended in 1688. It was owned for six generations by the family of Jacob Ege whose name appears on the Mayo map.

In April 1737 Colonel Byrd advertised in the *Virginia Gazette* that on the north side of James River, a little below The Falls, there had been " laid off by Major William Mayo, a town called Richmond, with streets sixty-five feet wide. A pleasant and healthy situation and well supplied with springs of good water. It is near the public Warehouse at Shockoes and in the midst of great quantities of Grain and all kinds of Provisions." The Act of Assembly incorporating the town is dated " May, 1742,

15 George II." It provides that two days annually in May, and two in November, shall be observed as " Fair Days, for the sale and vending of all manner of cattle, victuals, provisions, goods, wares and merchandise whatever."

This meant more than a mere market. It meant an opportunity and excuse for the coming together of the neighborhood for human intercourse. See them coming! In sloops—by the river—and over land—on horses, in carts or on foot. See them plodding over the clay hills and gullies—some driving livestock and with difficulty keeping it rounded up, others carrying hampers or sacks of home-made goods or farm produce on their own or their horses' backs, or in their carts. The young women are as smartly attired as they may be, the young farmers in such holiday clothes as they possess, for the Fair is an opportunity for exhibition of charms as well as of wares and there is no telling when a romance may date from a Fair Day. There are games of chance, and contests for prizes, and races. And strolling jesters, singers, dancers and performers on such musical instruments as the Jew's harp, the banjo and the fiddle take occasion to pick up a penny where they can.

Taverns are noisy and rowdy with jokes and laughter, drinking and gambling. There are some fights and some broken heads, but it is all for the most part merrily done, with no harm meant, and when quiet reigns once more and home folk and visitors to the Fair are settled down, none will be much worse off for the two days break in their routine. The *Virginia Gazette* gives this item, in May, 1774: " The subscription purse, £75, was run for at Richmond on the 12th inst., that being Fair Day, and was won by Mr. William Hardyman's sorrel mare."

Little more than seven years after the straggling settle-

THE VIRGINIA STATE CAPITOL ABOUT 1858
From an old print

WASHINGTON MONUMENT IN CAPITOL SQUARE
With a view of historic St. Paul's Church before its spire was removed

THE GOVERNOR'S HOUSE, IN CAPITOL SQUARE
Built 1810

THE BELL-TOWER IN CAPITOL SQUARE
Built in 1824 to succeed a frame structure on same site.   Spire of no-longer-existing First Presbyterian
Church in the distance.   From an old print

ment at The Falls had become a town, its founder and Father, Colonel William Byrd II, passed forever from the Virginia scene at " Westover ", like his father before him. He left his rôle and his property at The Falls to his only son, William Byrd III, who built a residence for occasional occupancy at Richmond. He chose a site far to the west of Richmond Hill and the checkerboard, and put upon it a commodious house with a two-storied, dormer-windowed central building and two one-storied dormer-windowed wings overlooking the river. It was fitly named " Belvidere " and a street of that name, a few blocks west of the Hill of the Grey Cross, identifies the location today.

In 1752, Richmond, in becoming the county seat, acquired some quaint appurtenances. Years earlier the Assembly had ordered, for Henrico, that " there being no Ducking Stool in the county as ye law enjoynes, Captain Thomas Cocke is requested and appointed . . . to erect one in some convenient place near ye court house." In addition to its jail, every county seat had its ducking-stool, its stocks, its pillory, and its whipping-post. Witches and scolding women were likely to be ducked, men guilty of all sorts of minor offenses condemned to the stocks, pillory or whipping-post.

To return to the Byrds, the third William had the distinguished appearance and attractive personality of his father and grandfather, without their business ability, energy and strength of character. In his hands the fortune which they had accumulated soon began to decay. The lottery was the cure-all of the day for financial troubles, and so in that summer of 1768 the new master of the Byrd estates advertised a " grand lottery " in which his lands at The Falls, including all improvements, were to be disposed of for 10,000 tickets at £5 each, 839 of which were to draw prizes. The drawing was quite an aristocratic affair, held under management of Presley Thornton, Peyton Randolph, John Page, Charles Carter and Charles Turnbull, Esquires. Some of the Byrd lottery tickets may still be found among old title deeds in Richmond.

Being sold by lottery does not seem to have retarded Richmond's progress, for the next year Shockoe Hill, across a valley through which flowed Shockoe Creek, was taken into its limits.

Hints in early eighteenth century letters and diaries suggest the beginnings of social life in the neighborhood of The Falls, even though it was on the dangerous frontier far from Jamestown and from the gay capital which Williamsburg was growing to be, with the coach and six, balls and the theatre, brocades and jewels becoming everyday matters. In 1701 Louis Michel, a Frenchman, on his way to the settlement of Huguenot refugees some distance above Richmond, visited Falling Creek and wrote in his diary: "We found good lodging places everywhere and since the people love strangers we had a good time." David Meade says in his autobiography, 1765: "The neighborhood of Curles, including that seat, abounded with as much beauty, fashion and rank as any part of Virginia." "Curles" plantation, named from the winding of the river at that point, was the seat of Richard Randolph, Jr., whose ancestor, William Randolph, had bought Bacon's confiscated property after the Rebellion. The neighborhood circle included, among others, sons and daughters of the house, their next neighbors, the Cockes of "Bremo", their cousins, the Carys of "Ampthill" and the Randolphs of "Wilton." At the time of which Meade writes Anne Randolph of the last named seat, known to her friends as "Nancy Wilton", was a reigning belle. Among her admirers was young Thomas Jefferson and among her lovers John Page of " Rosewell "—Governor of Virginia to be—and Benjamin Harrison, who finally married her and made her mistress of " Brandon." The country neighborhood of Richmond also included the Randolph family of " Tuckahoe ", another centre of hospitality and sociability, where Jefferson had lived during his schooldays. There are many evidences of growing trade. Ships that brought English goods to stores and homes went back laden with Virginia produce equally welcome on that side of the water. Among exports from Richmond and its neighborhood for the year from October 1764-1765 were over 20,000 hogsheads of tobacco, over 42,000 bushels of wheat, over 75,000 bushels of corn, much lumber and a quantity of iron. In 1766, 4,900 bushels of coal went over—doubtless from the mines in Chesterfield County across the river from Richmond. Thus Richmond and its neighborhood were helping to feed and shelter England as well as give it the solace of pipe dreams, and actually " sending coals to Newcastle."

In 1771 came the Great Freshet which nearly destroyed the growing town, but it pulled itself together pluckily, and was forging ahead again when the Revolution began to mutter.

PART II

THE REVOLUTION AND THE MAKING OF THE NATION

(1775-1790)

CHAPTER IV

" LIBERTY OR DEATH "

FOR ten years Virginia had been torn by dissension between a minority of her sons who regarded resistance to king and parliament as treason—no matter what the provocation—and the majority, who saw bowing to the will of a king and parliament, turned tyrants, as slavery. At firesides, in taverns, at county court-houses, around church doors, at the race, the cock-fight, the ball, men and women had wrangled over the rights of American subjects of the English king. A Convention to consider the subject had been held in the Capitol at Williamsburg, and now, on March 20, 1775, a second Convention was to meet, but a spot secure from interruption by the hostile royal governor, Lord Dunmore, was desired for it. The little town at The Falls seemed to offer such a retreat, but neither in the checkerboard nor among the sprinkling of houses beyond its limits was there an assembly-room large enough to hold the Convention—unless—unless the small white church in the green graveyard atop the hill could be made to serve! So it came to pass that the pews of St. John's were packed with a most novel congregation that spring day, and the dandelion-starred grass of the spaces between the tombstones and the open doors and windows of the tiny white church were trampled by the feet of a crowd of people who could not get inside, but were eager to see and to hear. The bell in the white steeple which had rung for services and tolled for funerals called the Convention together, but nobody knew that it was calling into being the American Revolution. From each county in Virginia two delegates—all of them locally prominent, some of them soon to win world fame—had made the toilsome journey to The Falls of James River. But they had never heard of steam or gasoline engines, nor been spoiled for rutty and miry roads by familiarity with those of macadam and concrete. Virginia—remember—extended then from the Atlantic Ocean to the Mississippi River, and included West Virginia and Kentucky. Delegates from distant frontier counties came on horseback carrying their belongings in saddlebags. The Virginian of the day was as much at home in his saddle as in his bed. Astride his horse he became a Centaur—he and his steed were one. On such a trip as this over mountain, down valley, across river, through forest, the saddle from sun-up till sundown and then, until sun-up again, bed in a tavern if he chanced to pass one, if not, in any farmhouse where he could find lodging, was the order of his going. He rode in his hunting clothes, well armed against attacks from Indian or bandit.

At St. John's, delegates were straggling in for a day or two. When all were in their seats and the roll was called, George Washington and Thomas Jefferson and Patrick Henry were among those to answer " Here l " and —to name a few more of them—Peyton Randolph, who presided, George Mason, Richard Henry Lee, George Wythe, Benjamin Harrison, Edmund Pendleton, Thomas Nelson, Jr., Richard Bland, Andrew Lewis, Robert Carter Nicholas, Archibald Cary, Carter Braxton, and others of equal or nearly equal calibre.

These men had come together for serious business and they knew it, but even as they sat tingling under the eloquence of a Patrick Henry they could not realize how solemn and memorable a scene they were enacting, with a church for a stage. Most of them were young or in their prime, with reputations as statesmen yet in the making. They did not look to one another or to the spectators like heroes in flesh and blood or like bronze figures. They were just men—calling one another George and Tom and Pat, and so on, ready to give or take a slap on the back accompanied by a joke and burst of spontaneous laughter in the wholesome, boyish way of Virginians from the beginning. Washington had not been married to the widow Custis long enough for the girls who had given him the mitten to be forgotten by gossip who (with all the world) loves a lover, nor Jefferson to the widow Skelton long enough for the figure he cut sighing disconsolately for " Belinda " to have ceased to be a subject for merriment, and we may be sure that every one of those embryo heroes in their queues and their cocked hats and their knee-buckles, assembled in St. John's spouting eloquence destined to be woven into the tapestry of American history had a story to tell on some other member. For what are men—the greatest of them—but grown-up boys? And not all of their recess-time was given to discussion of Convention matters. At taverns and private houses, tables were spread for them with ham, cabbage and corn-pones (food to the taste of every real Virginian—white or black), turkey, oysters, James River fish, mutton and venison, sweet and Irish potatoes, hominy and beans, pickles and preserves, jellies, puddings, pies, cakes—with toddy, punch, wine, beer and cider on the sideboard. When they had had their fill they made crowded rings around crackling log fires and with their pipes, their snuff-boxes or their quids—every man his tobacco to his liking—they stretched their legs in what space they could secure, took their ease after the tension of the session in St. John's, and talked, talked, talked! The smokers made the air thick. Now and again a snuff-taker almost raised the roof with his sneezes, or a chewer spat a mouthful of tobacco-juice into the heart of the fire. No, there was no bronze in their make-up. They were just human clay, though for some of them laurels were growing without knowing whose brows they would adorn, white marble was sleeping in the soil of Italy not dreaming whose shape it was destined to take, and apprentices in bronze foundries were learning their craft taking no thought of whose features they would one day portray.

Among recommendations passed by the Convention was one for continuing contributions for the relief of Boston. Patrick Henry's seat was in a pew (now bearing his name on a brass plate) near the east door. Memory of his great speech on his resolutions written on the fly-leaf of an old law-book and offered before the House of Burgesses at Williamsburg, in 1765, which (to use his own words), " formed the first opposition to the Stamp Act and scheme for taxing America by the British Parliament", was fresh and commanded close attention for every word he uttered. Early in the Convention he startled his hearers with his resolutions for raising an armed force for defense of Virginia. Many of the most patriotic among them believed this to be too radical a measure. It was long and passionately debated on both sides, and then, on the third day (to quote an eye-witness): " Henry arose with an unearthly fire burning in his eye. He commenced somewhat calmly—but the smothered excitement began more and more to play upon his features and thrill in the tones of his voice. The tendons of his neck stood out, white and rigid, like whip-cords. His voice rose louder and louder while the walls of the building and all within seemed to shake and rock in its tremendous vibrations. Finally, his pale face and glaring eyes became terrible to look upon. Men leaned forward

THE CAPITOL. CITY HALL IN CENTRAL BACKGROUND

HOUDON'S STATUE OF WASHINGTON

In the rotunda of the Capitol at Richmond. Made in 1785 by Houdon, the greatest sculptor of the time, who, at the invitation of Jefferson (acting for the State of Virginia) came from Paris to Mt. Vernon to model from Washington's person this portrait in white marble

in their seats with heads strained forward, their faces pale and their eyes glaring like the speaker's."

At length came the dramatic climax: " Is life so dear, is peace so sweet as to be purchased at the price of chains and slavery? Forbid it, Almighty God! I know not what course others may take; but as for me, give me liberty, or give me death!"

Says our witness: " When Mr. Henry sat down every eye yet gazed entranced " on him. " Men looked beside themselves . . . I felt sick with excitement."

Very different was the effect on a Tory who was present and who wrote to a friend of his own persuasion in Norfolk: " You never heard anything more infamously insolent than P. Henry's speech."

Following the speech a committee, with both Washington and Jefferson as members, adopted a plan for arming and equipping militia. Patrick Henry's burning words had resulted in pledging Virginia to war. On July 17th another Convention in St. John's planned further defense of the Colony and a temporary government. Now see the town at The Falls busying itself helping to take care of the army. Among Richmond advertisements the following May is one for " Journeymen weavers . . . also persons that can spin wool, linen or cotton." And in June: " Ten or twelve journeymen shoemakers are wanted, by Nicholas B. Seabrook, in Richmond Town." A woman who did her bit was Catherine Park whose husband made leather for the army. After his death she carried on his business and had hides tanned to make shoes for the soldiers.

Yet even in war-time ordinary life goes on. Three meals a day are eaten, the rite of dishwashing after them is performed, schools and shops function, the great human drama in three acts—birth, marriage, death—is enacted.

RICHMOND: ITS PEOPLE AND ITS STORY

We find in the *Gazette* a "doctoress and midwife"
advertising for business, in Richmond; a school-mistress
announcing "a boarding-school for young ladies . . to
instruct them in reading, writing and arithmetic, the French
language . . . and different kinds of needlework", including "the tambour"; and James Galt "clock and
watchmaker and jeweler" of Williamsburg proclaims his
intention to remove to "Richmond Town", where he will
"keep clocks in repair by the year at reasonable rates."

So while the cloud the size of a man's hand which
the Stamp Act had brought over the sea, and which everybody in America now knew to be a war-cloud, thickened
and spread—thickened and spread, hall clocks and mantel
clocks in homes at The Falls cosily and correctly checked
off the portentous minutes as if they had been ordinary
minutes of any other time. When they struck twelve on
the night of June 26, 1776, the Williamsburg Convention
had adopted a constitution for England's first colony as
an independent state, and appointed Patrick Henry its
first governor. The news made a gala day for Richmond
Town, but not until August 5th "being a court day"—
was the Declaration of Independence proclaimed there.
"It was received", says our amiable gossip, the *Gazette*,
"with universal shouts of joy and re-echoed by three
vollies of small arms." "The same evening the town
was illuminated, and the members of the Committee held
a club when many patriotic toasts were drunk. Although
there were nearly one thousand people present the whole
was conducted with the utmost decorum and the satisfaction visible in every countenance evinces their determina-
tion to support it with their lives and fortunes." With
their lives and fortunes! Richmond men were soon sup-
porting the American cause with their lives—proud that

34

leadership had fallen upon Virginia's own Washington— Richmond women practising severest self-denial to provide the men at the front with necessities, while they waited with anxious hearts the slow-footed news. Many a mother, sister, sweetheart or wife counted the strokes of the clock in the night as she wondered if " his " letter would ever come to tell her how " he " fared on battle-field, march, or in camp. Every traveler, by horseback, foot, stage, or sloop was hailed with joy for the tidings he might bring. The hard times that are a part of war times became acute. On what was then Broad Road, but is now Broad Street (near Tenth Street), lived the accomplished Dr. James Currie—probably in a quaint, rambling house which was lately pulled down. There were then no medical ethics to prevent his advertising in the *Gazette* that his " fees for the practice of physick " would be " at the old rates, before the exorbitant prices of medicine as well as every necessity of life made it equitable to raise them." Dr. William Foushee, for whom Foushee Street is named, but whose home, with its office and garden was then on Main Street, on the site of the present post-office, announced that his charges would be " as formerly "—namely " a visit in town in the day five shillings, an emetic two shillings, six pence ; either in commodities that he needs, or in tobacco at 20 shillings per hundred weight, or money." Virginia physicians had long to content themselves with pay chiefly in " commodities."

A welcome visitor was a schooner appropriately named *Good Intent* which ran the blockade and made port at Richmond about Christmas 1776. Joshua Storrs, Hugh Walker & Company, sold to the neighborhood storekeepers her cargo from the West Indies, consisting of " gunpowder, nails, osnaburgs, white linen, men's and women's white silk hose, needles, pins and writing paper. Also, a few hogsheads of rum and molasses." Of course the "public vendue" of this intriguing "assortment of dry-goods" put all Richmond and its neighborhood in a flutter. A cheering letter for Colonel William Aylett, Deputy Commissary General of Virginia, told him that Mr. Richard Adams, of Richmond had engaged at Overton's Mill in that town five hundred barrels of flour "for use of the Army." But money and supplies grew scarcer and scarcer.

CHAPTER V

RICHMOND BECOMES VIRGINIA'S CAPITAL

WILLIAMSBURG, being so near the seaboard, was constantly exposed to the enemy, and, besides, its situation had ceased to be desirable as the capital of a state whose settlements had extended beyond the Alleghanies. In May, 1779, the Assembly, acting on a suggestion made by Jefferson several years before, decided to remove the capital to Richmond, because it was " more safe and central than any other town situated on navigable water." The Act provided for a handsome State House and Halls of Justice—with walls of brick or stone, porticoes wherever they might be found convenient or ornamental, with pillars and pavement of brick or stone—and for wooden buildings for immediate use. The Assembly appointed a board of directors for the town (with Jefferson as its head) which met at Hoggs Tavern, in August, and planned a temporary Capitol at the northwest corner of the present Cary and Fourteenth Streets. The General Assembly met in it in the following May and promptly passed " An Act creating the Public Square, to enlarge the town of Richmond, widening the streets, making Shockoe Creek navigable " (so that boats could " come up to the warehouse landing for the benefit of the public ") and providing a public market place. The present Capitol Square and Old Market are memorials of this Act.

Becoming Virginia's capital meant a big stride forward for the town at The Falls. Norfolk and one or two other towns in the state were larger. By comparison with elegant Williamsburg (with its mile-long Duke of Gloucester Street, its Palace Green, its century-old mansions, its shrubberies and over-arching trees, and its seat of learning, William and Mary College), Richmond was still a village and a crude one—for all its schooners being loaded and unloaded at the riverfront by laughing, singing negroes, its warehouses filled with tobacco and other produce for export, its semi-annual fairs and its checkerboard of streets. These last were deep in dust when the sun shone, or in slippery red-clay mud when there was rain. Goats sported and hogs rooted in them, and cows munched the grass and buttercups that found a foothold in their soil. In pleasant weather ebon-skinned washer-women, in homespun dresses with gay colored handkerchiefs tied around their heads, scrubbed clothes in the creek which made up between Church Hill and Shockoe Hill, and hung them out to dry on its grassy margin—monotonously chanting after their fashion as they worked. Winds blew the weird sounds about until they were lost in the roar of The Falls. In this same Shockoe Creek geese and ducks paddled and, in summertime, boys learned to swim.

Most of the houses in the checkerboard were of wood —one-story and a dormer or two stories and a dormer— with heavy shutters and chimneys built of short logs chinked with clay. And with an outside kitchen and smoke-house and perhaps a one-story office for the master of the house. If he happened to be a merchant, the lower part of the house was his store and the rooms above were his home.

In becoming the capital, Richmond became the home of Jefferson who had succeeded Henry as Governor. He had always been a familiar figure in the neighborhood, first in boyhood when he lived at "Tuckahoe" (a few miles up the river), in his college days when he made one of the train of charming Nancy Randolph at "Wilton"

SWAN TAVERN

MASONIC HALL
The oldest Masonic Hall in continuous use in America, built 1785

RICHMOND IN 1796, FROM A SKETCH BY B. H. LATROBE

RICHMOND IN 1798, FROM A PAINTING BY PLEASANTS
The painting owned by the Misses Stewart, of "Brook Hill"

and later, as man. Of course, all latch-strings hung on the outside of the door for him. Another addition to the town's importance was a semi-weekly newspaper, for that storehouse of cheerful gossip—that paper with a personality, the *Virginia Gazette*, also moved from Williamsburg to Richmond. In its garrulous way, it tells of a group of " likely " negroes to be sold for cash, loan office certificate or tobacco, among whom is "as good a cook as any in Virginia." Gruesome—yet read perhaps a little wistfully by ye modern housewife.

Although the seven years war of the Revolution was rung in at Richmond, it was not until the year when that town became the capital that The Falls of James River had a glimpse of British Red Coats. Some officers of Burgoyne's Army, captured at the battle of Saratoga, were sent there to be quartered, on parole, in private homes. The impressions of one of these unusual guests remain in a little book entitled *Anburey's Travels*. The author describes " Belvidere " (then the Harvie home) at which he was quartered as " an elegant villa . . . as romantic and elegant as anything I have ever seen." He says " Many gentlemen around Richmond, though strongly attached to the American cause, have shown the liberality and hospitality so peculiar to this province in their particular attention and civilities to our officers. Among those who are most distinguished in this line are Colonel Randolph, of ' Tuckahoe', Colonel Goode, of Chesterfield, and Colonel Cary of ' Ampthill'." The rougher element did not fancy such graciousness toward enemy officers. One of them became so enraged on seeing Doctor Foushee showing the Red Coats about town that he attacked that beloved physician and gouged out one of his eyes.

In the last year of the war—1781—the traitor Benedict Arnold with some eight hundred infantry and a small detachment of the Queen's Rangers sailed into James River and included Richmond in a series of unwelcome New Year's calls. Landing at the home of the founder of Richmond, fair " Westover ", he feasted his men and horses and set out toward the town itself. Early the next afternoon—January 5th—the Red Coats marched up Main street, drums beating, banners flying, gay uniforms lighting up the street. Richmond was utterly unprepared for their visit. The only semblance of American soldiery there were a couple of hundred raw, poorly equipped militia, who were hurriedly corralled and drawn up on Chimborazo Hill, beyond St. John's, and a few mounted men who were as hurriedly stationed on the brow of Shockoe Hill, at about Fifth Street. General Nelson, with a handful of militia, badly supplied with ammunition, had marched up the opposite bank of the river, but arrived too late to offer resistance to the British.

While General Arnold was marching up Main Street his capable subordinate, Colonel Simcoe, at the head of the Queen's Rangers, went after the militia on Chimborazo. When the militia saw what was coming, they decided to a man, to live to fight another day, and skedaddled. The Rangers galloped back to Main Street, by which they ascended Shockoe, and put the little troop of cavalry there to flight—after capturing a few good horses. With these to aid them, they made a dash for Westham Foundry (above The Falls), put the cannon there out of commission, destroyed the small arms and threw five tons of gunpowder into the river. Governor Jefferson, in an attempt to save the public stores, had part of them removed across the river opposite Westham. On the night of January 4th, when Arnold had been encamped at Four Mile Creek, below Richmond, preparatory to entering town next day, the Governor was at " Tuckahoe ", ten or twelve miles above town. Next day he went across the river to Colonel Fleming's to meet and confer with Baron Steuben (then in command of Virginia troops), and while there received a message from Arnold saying that he would not burn Richmond if British vessels were permitted to come up and take tobacco from the warehouses unmolested. The offer was declined, but there really was nobody to molest a thousand Red Coats, and from his point of vantage across the river, in Manchester, the Governor had to bear with what grace he could muster seeing public and private property seized, public buildings and records burned. Much captured liquor went down the throats of the invaders. What they could not swill or carry off they poured into the streets. The hogs riotously rooted in the unique mire it made until swine and men reeled and staggered against one another while the looting and burning went on.

History repeats itself. War is, was, and always will be—" Hell."

To give the devil his due, be it said that Arnold did not carry out his threat to make a bonfire of the defenseless and panic-stricken town. Among the things he did burn was a large amount of paper money, freshly printed, and not yet issued. Cheap as it was, it was better than no money. He also burned much tobacco, which was real money, for the tobacco note was currency in Virginia from early Colonial days until long after the Revolution, and to destroy the tobacco was to make the tobacco note worthless. About midday, January 6th, the Red Coats marched down Main Street again and back to " Westover." To relieve the situation in Virginia General Washington now sent the gallant young Marquis de la Fayette with some Continental troops to form a junction with Baron Steuben, and take command. He reached Richmond in April. On April 27th Arnold, who had joined his forces with those of General Phillips, sunk or captured almost all of the small Virginia navy at Coxendale, not far below Richmond, and turned his face again toward The Falls. At Manchester more tobacco was burned, but news of the presence of the Marquis and his blue and buff battalions in Richmond made the Red Coats decide that it was their turn to prove that discretion was the better part of valor. On May 17th Lafayette was encamped at " Wilton." When Lord Cornwallis advanced toward him by way of Petersburg with eight thousand troops—a very superior force—the Marquis retreated. Cornwallis with his eight thousand dashed after him, but soon gave up, leaving Tarleton and his cavalry to continue the chase. Tarleton pursued Lafayette to beyond Fredericksburg, when he too, gave up and fell back toward Richmond.

Lafayette, in his rapid retreat from Richmond, made a new road known to this day as " the Marquis's road." On June 15th, he was reinforced by General Wayne's regular troops from the Pennsylvania Continental line, sent to Virginia for the purpose, and advanced again toward Richmond Town. But Cornwallis was ahead of him. Entering the town on June 16th, he gave his troops a few days' rest and opportunity to pillage and forage before beginning his retreat down the peninsula between James and York Rivers. Lafayette and his forces—including the Pennsylvania troops—passed through Richmond in pursuit of Cornwallis on June 22d—just twenty-four hours after the enemy left, leaving the town " a scene of much distress." Lafayette and his forces overtook and attacked Cornwallis (unsuccessfully) near Jamestown, on July 6th, after which he fell back to " Malvern Hill ", where he camped for the protection of Richmond. In this month an unexpected and ghastly foe, General Small-pox, captured the desperate little capital.

RICHMOND IN 1800
From an old engraving

JOHN MARSHALL, CHIEF JUSTICE OF THE UNITED STATES
From the portrait by Inman, Virginia State Library

RICHMOND BECOMES VIRGINIA'S CAPITAL

When Washington and the French troops began the Allied movement toward Yorktown Lafayette marched from his post below Richmond down the peninsula, while the Pennsylvania troops, which had been stationed on the south side of the river, crossed at Westham, passing through town on August 8th. It seems that the last American troops on their way to meet the enemy seen by Richmond and its neighborhood were Wayne's Pennsylvanians, for Washington's Army, on its way to Yorktown, passed east of and not through the town. And now Richmond, with all Virginia, is filled with hope that the great combined American and French movement may result in capture of the British Army and end of war. All aglow over the happy turn of the tide, Governor Nelson—who had succeeded Jefferson—writes from Richmond to Governor Burke of North Carolina, telling him of the arrival of Count de Grasse, and that General Washington, " with all the French troops of the Northern Army and a body of Continentals, is on the march for Virginia." An earlier version of " Over there " was in the air of Richmond and its neighborhood though it was not set to music:

" The French are coming! "

The French are coming! was the joyous thought of every patriot heart. And, in that dark hour, it was the French who hastened the dawn for Americans just as, in poetic justice, Americans hastened it for Frenchmen nearly a century and a half later. Fortunately Richmond understood that the allied army coming nearer and nearer every day, to bring deliverance and peace, was but a horde of hungry men. To save Virginia's reputation for hospitality they must be fed. In common humanity they must be fed. To bring deliverance they must be fed—and they were fed. Richmond was the centre from which supplies for the allied armies were directed, and many of them were provided by Richmond Town and its neighborhood. Among letters which brought Governor Nelson relief in this great anxiety was one from John Pierce telling him of shipments down the river of flour for the allied troops and adding that he expected "more every minute from Westham."

Just who brought the news of the surrender at Yorktown to Richmond is not known, but we may be sure he owned the town that day. Maybe it was Colonel William Fontaine, who was there and just a week later wrote a friend a letter from Richmond describing it, which concludes: "I enclose two yards of ribbon for my sister Sarah and two for sister Mary, or, in her absence little Bess—trophies from York."

Virginia was free of Red Coats, the boys whose letters were so slow were coming home in person, and Richmond Town was gay with meetings and greetings, yet it was still—with difficulty—doing its bit to provide for the still fighting army in South Carolina; with difficulty—for history repeats itself and war times were followed by hard times. How the Governor must have hated to see his mail bag brought in! Its contents were clamorous with appeals of men struggling with the problem of making bricks without straw, for the public treasury, like private purses, was empty. A fair sample of these letters was one about New Year, from Major Richard Claiborne, who could not send a quantity of clothing, spirits and medicine (which was waiting in Richmond) to General Greene's Army in the South because there was not a wagon in condition to travel and the horses were lean and poor. He had tried "every blacksmith shop around to get the wagons fixed and the horses shod", but "with contempt they refuse striking their hammers without the money is paid down." Charles Russell, Quartermaster of Manchester, reported that the

44

RICHMOND BECOMES VIRGINIA'S CAPITAL

Continental horses were starving. Other public servants declared they could not continue in office without means to meet the high cost of living in Richmond. Major John Pryor, when asked to suggest a man for a military service facetiously named " Mr. Royall, who possesses the art of living without money." In 1783 David Ross, a leading merchant of Richmond, prayed to be paid for furnishing the Southern Army with " near one thousand worth of supplies at a very critical and distressing period." His only pay had been General Greene's letter of thanks. Desperate deeds were a result of the hard times—history repeats itself. The tiny jail was packed to suffocation, and as prisoners were sentenced to death not only for murder, but for burglary; horse-stealing, treason and other offences, public hangings offered frequent and popular entertainment.

In the midst of so much trouble the place was going ahead. War was ended though peace had not been proclaimed. Richmond Town received its charter as a city in May, 1782. Twelve of its citizens were chosen to form a Common Hall, which elected Dr. William Foushee, Mayor, and Mr. William Hay, Recorder—or City Judge. It also granted Mr. Ryan, manager of the theatre, permission to renew his license. His playhouse was only a shanty on lower Main Street, but it is refreshing to know that the people had even that in those bleak times. There were other diversions too. An occasional wedding gave opportunity for people to forget their troubles in witnessing the ever fresh scene from real life of love's young dream come true, which turned even hardest times into times of rejoicing. And there were always feet eager to dance in Richmond, and darkies as eager to play the fiddle, pick the banjo and call the figures.

Among after-the-war tourists to Richmond was Dr.

Johann Schoepf, a Hessian, who had served in the British Army. His diary shows him to have been grouchy and prejudiced but a keen observer. The Assembly was in session and " The coming together of so many gentlemen from all parts of the province brought hither a great number of fine horses. One could almost fancy it was an Arabian village. There were to be seen the whole day long saddled horses at every turn and a swarming of riders in the few and muddy streets, for a horse must be mounted, if only to fetch a pinch of snuff from across the way."

All of the inns were crowded. " Assemblymen, judges, doctors, clerks and gentlemen of every weight and calibre and every line of dress sat all together about the fire, drinking, smoking, singing and telling stories." " In the same clothes in which one goes hunting or tends his tobacco fields it is permissible to appear in the Senate or the Assembly. There are displayed trousers, stockings, and Indian leggings, great coats, ordinary coats, and short jackets, according to each man's caprice or comfort, and all equally honorable." In contrast are his pictures of Virginia women, whom he finds " clothed and adorned with great fastidiousness." On his way to Richmond, when stopping for a night at a tavern—" a draughty, empty place ", where " neither rum nor whisky nor bread was to be bought "— he had the " unexpected pleasure " of making his "devoirs" to " several ladies dressed tastefully in silk and decked with plumes." (They were evidently on their way for a visit at some plantation or town, and stopping to rest themselves and their horses, as he was. Their finery was probably bought before the war, for silk was made to last in those days). At Hanover Court House, nearer Richmond, he found " On a very warm midday, a fine circle of ladies, silk-clad and tastefully coiffured, sitting about the fire. This was not so extraordinary in itself, but it

46

was something new to me that several pretty vigorous young blacks, quite in their natural state, should be tumbling about before the party without scandal." (They were doubtless clad in the cotton smocks worn by negro children in warm weather). Writing of "the want of hard money", he says: "Tobacco pays their taxes, gives the women their indispensable silks and laces . . . . and everything which is not produced at home." And of the king's English as he heard it spoken in Richmond: "Virginians boast that among all the American Colonies the English language is with them preserved purest and most complete, and one cannot altogether deny them. But here and there a few negroisms have crept in and the salmagundi of the English language has here been enriched by even words of African origin."

CHAPTER VI

PEACE DECLARED

PEACE at last! And peace at the most fitting of all times, the approach of Christmas. The Treaty which meant definite ending of the war had been signed and the good news had reached The Falls of James River. Peace on earth was a fact. America—Virginia—Richmond needed no other Christmas gift. What difference did poverty make? *Peace on earth, good will toward men!* The bell in the white steeple of St. John's on the Hill flung out the words. The Falls shouted them. Even the tavern bells calling guests from their beds or to their meals seemed to repeat them. The laughter of children echoed them. *Peace on earth!* The kisses of young love were sweeter for it, the eyes of old folks shone with it, the voices of men of affairs and their wives were hearty with it, the hand-clasp of friendship was warm with it. The mantel clocks and the hall clocks seemed to tick more happily the minutes of peace and when they chimed the hours —to foretell many happy years. After all the drab Christmases of war time, Christmas was new in Richmond that year, Christ was born again. *Peace on earth, good will toward men!* Young negroes cut the pigeon-wing and jumped juba in the streets and old ones went about giving one another the " right hand of fellowship ", with " Howdy Brother! Howdy Sister! Bless de Lord!"

At sundown, the day news of the Treaty came, Richmond windows began to bloom with lighted candles. Every home was bright with as many of them as its owner could afford, and such fireworks as could be procured were made to echo " Peace on earth, good will toward men!" As soon

48

as arrangements could be made there was a ball at the Capitol. No social lines were drawn. Equality was the popular slogan. America was a republic now. Down with rank! It must be everybody's ball, and everybody must come and dance. Who should lead it? In former times that honor would have belonged as a right to a lady of the Governor's household, but the Revolution had blotted out rank. The only thing that would give every lady an equal chance was a lottery. Every lady and girl drew, and many a heart fell as its owner found she had drawn a blank. Finally a young girl who had bashfully taken her turn, tremulously showed her slip. It held the magic sign! All eyes were turned on her. She blushed as if she had committed a sin. For—oh, the wonder of it!—She, a shoemaker's daughter, had drawn a thing which would give her, for a night, precedence over all the belles of Richmond Town! Out of the buzz of talk it made came unanimous decision that her claim was valid. She led the Peace Ball.

The happiest event of that happy New Year came the next autumn when General Washington and the Marquis de la Fayette visited Richmond at the same time—arriving there several days apart. The Assembly, then in session, sent each of them in turn an address of welcome—with Patrick Henry as chairman and James Madison as a member of each presentation committee. A great dinner was given them at The Bell Tavern and the town and the visiting Assemblymen turned out and escorted them to it. In an old letter it is written: "The presence of General Washington and the Marquis has kept the city alive for near a week past. Feasting, balls, illuminations and firing of cannon etc., etc., has been our chief employment since the Generals came to town."

Richmond was gradually getting back to normality and was reaching out to the outside world.

In 1785 a regular post was established to and from Norfolk and Portsmouth, by way of Suffolk, and soon afterward the Southern Stage line, with four horses to each stage was running to Wilmington, North Carolina, where its passengers could change to a packet boat for Charleston, South Carolina.

There were as yet in Richmond but three or four hundred houses and four thousand inhabitants, counting white and black. The Old Dominion was one of large plantations and small towns. A surprising number of the houses must have been stores over which lived their proprietors, according to custom. Announcements in the yellowed pages of the *Gazette* for 1785 and 1786 show frequent arrival of ships from European ports bringing wares to be exchanged with these merchants for tobacco. Only the smaller of the ships came all the way to Richmond. The larger ones lay in the river below and the announcements provide us with the names of the merchants and lists of their fascinating wares. Also, they indicate that, along with other generals, General Prosperity was well on the way to Richmond and its neighborhood. Houses were not numbered in the advertisements and description of shops had to be given. Like this: "The green painted store near the Capitol", and this: "Lewis Ganot's Store, the west side of the Bridge, the opposite corner to Mr. Banks' Store." And this: "William Waddell, Goldsmith & Jeweller at the Sign of the Thirteen Stars opposite Mr. Anderson's Tavern." Mr. Waddell's large and varied stock "to be sold for cash, tobacco or State Security", included "jewelry, paste shoe-buckles, and knee-buckles, gold and silver watches, plated spurs, and Wilton Carpeting." "Mourning rings, hair devices" and engraving were furnished on order. A suitable sign for most of the shops would have been "Dry Goods and Wet Goods", for whatever they did

or did not have for sale there is always a list of drink-
ables. Joseph Darmstadt has " Just imported old Jamaica
spirits, sugar, coffee, gin in bottles. Also, a neat assortment of drygoods suitable to the season." " Wright and
Southgate " offer " A great assortment of East India and
European goods ", including " Superfine and Second
broadcloths of various colors . . . Corduroys, velvets,
plushes and hair shags . . . Camblets, taminies, durants,
russets, calimancoes, black crapes and bombazines . . .
Ladies and gentlemen's great coats with satin and velvet
capes . . . Scarlet, crimson, black, and drab cloth coats
trimmed with gimp and ermine. Ladies muffs and tippets
with a great variety of broad and narrow ermines . . .
Silk and satin quilted coats of all colors some made for
hoops . . . Bell hoops and ladies Italian stays . . . Mus-
lins, plain, striped, sprig, and checked . . . Gentlemen's
Bristol stone knee-buckles and sleeve-buckles . . . Drab
colored silks for gentlemen's summer coats . . . ladies
riding hats trimmed with feathers . . . Satin and cali-
manco shoes . . . Children's toy books ", etc., and " Old
Jamaica spirits by the hogshead, cognac brandy by the
pipe, old claret, Burgundy and Muscadel wines by the case
or dozen." Connor and Gernon have " Just imported from
France "—among other things "—" Elegant lute strings
and satins, silk handkerchiefs, silk stockings, ribands, sewing silk, feathers, artificial flowers, garlands, white and
colored kid gloves for ladies and gentlemen, paste neck-
laces, puffs and hair powder, pomatum and perfumes, elegant double gilt looking-glasses . . . hyson tea, single,
double and refined sugar, muscat and frontignac wines,
Margaux claret in cases of three dozen bottles, cordial,
apricots and plums preserved in syrup, apple, cherry and
quince jellies in pots of one pound each, chocolate, oil in
flasks, anchovies, Capers and Cognac brandy seven years

old." Interesting items in the long list of things " just imported " by Boyd and White are: " Ladies hunting saddles . . . tortoise shell and horn crooked combs . . . violins and bows . . . rich florentines for waistcoats and breeches . . . Persian bonnets and hats ", and " rich Persian and satin quilts." Hollingsworth, Johnson and Company give a dash of the variety that is the spice of life, with their " Leghorn hats, Windsor chairs and an elegant light chariot and two phaetons ", and John Barret and Company add still more of that spice with their " Elegant and extensive assortment of London made mahogany furniture ", their " plain and figured silk purses, wafers, sealing wax and best Dutch quills ", and " a few patterns of elegant paper tapestry for rooms." James Warrenton strikes a newer note still with his " Lady's clogs " (wooden overshoes), " elegant ostrich feathers, black and white . . . men and women's black lamb, white kid, wash leather, beaver, silk, holland and jeans gloves . . . gold and silver wove buttons, plain and fancy, gold and silver bindings and fringes, gold and silver cords, point lace, shaving pouches fitted with instruments complete . . . approved patent medicines in great variety . . . best London editions (of books) elegantly bound . . . lute and octave harpsichords with pedal swell . . . very best piano fortes . . . guitars, violins, new music and instructions by the most approved masters . . . patent floor cloths without a seam—Indian patterns . . . gentlemen's waistcoat patterns embroidered in gold." John and Joseph Henry, in a list of over a hundred items—" and a number of articles too tedious to mention "—name " Harry and Merry Andrew playing cards, Men's cocked and roundbeaver hats, white and brown do, with green under, ladies and gentlemen's saddlery in the newest taste elegantly mounted, ink powder, Jew's harps, snuff boxes ", and, of course, liquors. The only sales of absolutely " dry " goods seem to have been the frequent book auctions which were generally held in taverns, where if anything wet should be needed to wash down the classics it was easily procurable. Mr. Galt had plenty of competition in supplying Time to the people of Richmond when " John Reilly, watch-maker from Dublin", opened shop, and John Humphreys promised to " make and repair musical, repeating and plain clocks ", and sell " repeating, horizontal, and plain watches ", while John Wilson offered " tortoise-shell watches " and " watches that show the day of the month."

Reading the elaborate lists of things " just imported " the wonder grows where purchasers for all these goods were found. Wealthy planters for miles around went ashopping to Richmond Town and stores in smaller settlements laid in their stocks there. The Jockey Club races, held three days in May and September, and the dancing " Assemblies " which were regularly held after New Year 1785, gave excuse for buying the finery offered by the shops, and opportunity for displaying it. The year following had the added diversions of an " elegant ball " at the Capitol, to celebrate Washington's birthday, an " elegant dinner " on the Fourth of July, and a gathering in Richmond of the Virginia Cincinnati—which meant much entertaining and excited donning of the best bib and tucker. And of course there was church. It is written that in 1785, " a numerous and respectable meeting of Quakers assembled at the Capitol " and " two eminent female speakers from Boston held forth."

As to the attire of the audience of these grey ladies the witness is silent, but Dr. Thomas Coke, the noted Methodist Missionary who preached in the Capitol two years later, recorded that the " most dressy congregation he had seen in America " came to hear him. Among merchants who have not been mentioned were Pennock and Skipwith (who carried on a large business), Scott and Benge, Drinkel and Prentis, Buchanan and McKeand, Mr. Bently, Matthew Wright, James Lowell—who had at his store "at the foot of Shockoe Hill" an alluring stock, including "Chests of drawers and dressing glasses, oval and square, tea and card tables, gilt looking glasses, and warming pans." Many of these merchants were Scotchmen. Cohen and Isaacs were proprietors of "The Jews' Store", and there was a Jewish broker—Levi Israel. A German chandler, Meyer Dinkheim, moulded "candles— the light of the time—for 1 cent per pound", while a French dentist, Dr. Le Mayeur, reversed the usual order of things by "putting in natural teeth instead of false." Among physicians (all of whom furnished drugs to their patients and some of whom also kept drug stores), were "Dr. Gibson, near the Capitol", "James Francis Conand, Surgeon-Doctor, near the Bridge", and "William and Thomas Carter, Doctors and Surgeons."

In December 1785, Patrick Henry again became Governor of Virginia and a resident of Richmond. Perhaps it was to celebrate his election that Monsieur Busselot, on a bright winter's day, gave a free for all entertainment by sending up from the Capitol Square a balloon which "ascended a great height and descended on the plantation of Captain John Austin ten miles distant." This to spectators unspoiled by the feats of modern birdmen, seemed quite as wonderful as the great dirigibles of today do to us. Quite modern looking headlines scream from the old pages of the *Gazette*: "WE WANT A COOK!" and our sympathies are further appealed to by the plaint of a gentleman whose "wife Sarah" has "left him without any provocation." The Fellowship Fire Company was doing its best to protect property with a formally organized bucket brigade. This did valiant service in 1787, when the Fire Fiend destroyed forty or fifty buildings in the heart of town, including Anderson's Tavern and Byrd's Warehouse, with seventy hogsheads of tobacco.

In the spring of 1786, Alexander Quarrier " Coach Maker from Philadelphia ", set up shop in Richmond, and announced in the *Gazette* that he would " receive orders from any part of the United States." Among others advertising fine vehicles for sale are James Brown with his " elegant post chaise lately imported with harness compleat for six horses ", and Major Pryor with his " riding and carriage horses and sundry very elegant chariots and phaetons ", at Haymarket Stables.

These wares were needed—not only for driving about the hilly, and by turns dusty and muddy town and its neighborhood—but visiting distant towns and plantations was a favorite diversion, and Richmond people were making summer trips to the Springs. An advertisement of the " Sweet Springs "—still a popular resort—gives directions for carriage routes and describes accommodations: " A good two story house with eight lodging rooms and a number of log huts with plank floors rendered as comfortable as such buildings made in haste will admit." Primitive, but the swimming pool, medicinal waters, and mountain scenery made them endurable. Doubtless before setting out, many of the guests made visits to Major Pryor's Stables and had their horses " elegantly nicked for a guinea each, by Nicholas Atkinson ", by whom also " cropping and foxings in the neatest styles " and " all kinds of farriery ", were " performed on the most reasonable terms and with the greatest dispatch." In Richmond and its neighborhood not to know Major John Pryor of the Revolution was to argue one's self unknown. He was a judge of horse flesh and Secretary of the Jockey Club, a good fellow and an all round sport. He doubtless exhibited at the races the smartest of curled and queued locks, the

jauntiest of " just imported " cocked hats, the bravest of
gold embroidered waistcoats. He gave Richmond its first
recreation park—where Byrd Street Station now stands—
and here is his advertisement for a concessionaire to run
a tavern in connection with it: " To be rented a large commodious Inn on Haymarket Square contiguous to my livery
stables with a garden and suitable out houses; its situation
being a little remote from the noise and dust of the town
and commanding a delightful prospect of The Falls and
country adjacent to the city will render it a handsome retreat for parties to regale themselves with Ice, Punch,
Creams, &c. The Ice house being nearly completed, a
Billiard house is also erecting in the yard. To an active
person that will certainly keep the above place in elegant
and orderly manner a great bargain will be given."

But the town at The Falls was not altogether given
over to play. In the cause of culture the Richmond Library
announced hours when subscribers could " draw books ", a
" young lady capable of instructing in reading, writing, and
needlework desired a place as governess in a genteel family ", and a number of schools were advertised, among them
that of Mr. W. V. Worn, who in addition to a day school
conducted a practical "evening school" where " reading,
writing, arithmetic and bookkeeping were taught " and that
of Mr. " Eldridge Harris, of the Petersburg Academy "
which offered instruction in " Latin, Greek, and a gram-
matical knowledge of the English language, with Geography, writing, arithmetic, etc. " It remained for a Frenchman to render stale and colorless in the eyes of Richmond
youth the conventional methods of these staid school-
masters. For Monsieur Quesnay announced the opening
of an " Academy next door to Captain Michaell's, opposite
the Bridge ", where " drawing, French, music, etc.", would
be taught in the forenoon and dancing in the afternoon.
There was to be " a private school for gentlemen at night ",

and soon, " an assembly where ladies and gentlemen can practice dancing together." In December he announced that only three afternoons in the week would be given to dancing, the other days to be given entirely to " drawing, painting, music, and foreign languages, geography, astronomy, writing and arithmetic." Both young gentlemen and young ladies were to be admitted—and " good boarding houses " to be opened for young ladies. In a very depressed announcement in January he complains that " the disposition of minds in every place he has attempted educational work in America, are inclined to encourage nothing but dancing " and gives notice that he will leave Richmond at the end of the session.

But there was soon a turn of the tide. In June following, the corner stone of the Academy building was laid, with Masonic rites, on " Academy Square ", near the site of the present Monumental Church. Through the *Gazette*, Monsieur Quesnay expressed gratitude for patronage and announced the arrival from England of " globes, all kinds of patterns for drawing and painting, a complete collection of statues of plaster of Paris, all kinds of paints and patterns for landskip painting, instruments of music and music books." Mr. R. Morris would " teach the young ladies tambour, embroidery and all kinds of needle work, also vocal music." " Both living and dead languages " were to be taught. The building had a hall designed to be rented out to theatrical companies from time to time, and thus earn money for the benefit of the Academy. As soon as this hall was completed, in the early fall, Hallam and Henry played in it. The night of December 7, 1787, was a gala occasion, when society in its smartest attire was called out by a performance of " The Beggar's Opera ", in the Academy Hall, described as the " New Theatre on Shockoe Hill."

CHAPTER VII

THE CONVENTION OF '88

A MORE thrilling drama than any of poet's dream was soon to be enacted within the Academy's walls. The seven years' war was seven years past. The thirteen colonies were thirteen free states. Yet there was no real union, for there was no national government. The great majority of the people did not want a national government. They had thrown off government turned tyrant; they feared that in time a new government might turn tyrant also, that it might mean a yoke heavier than the one they had fought to be rid of—a yoke of unbearable taxes. True, the Philadelphia Convention had draughted a Constitution and America's idol, Washington—as President of the Convention—had signed it, and ardently desired its ratification. But ratification meant national government, and many of the wisest as well as many of the wildest believed that national government would endanger dear-bought liberty. Liberty was the word to conjure with—liberty confused in the minds of the mob with license. Anarchy was rife. (How history repeats itself!) Some of the states had ratified, with narrow majorities, after hard-fought, bitter battles, but the Constitution hung in the balance, perilously near defeat. Virginia had not spoken. Virginia, with its extensive area, its rich resources, its population larger than that of the proud states of New York and Massachusetts combined. Virginia had rung in the Revolution. Virginia would be the field where the decisive battle would be fought. As Virginia voted, the Constitution would stand or fall.

A convention to consider ratification was called to

meet in Richmond. It met in the new Academy Hall on June 2, 1788. In every Virginia county from those of far Kentucky (which sent fourteen delegates), to those in the immediate neighborhood of Richmond, feeling ran high and election of delegates created local tempests. Wherever two or more men met in any part of the state the Constitution was the subject of excited conversation or bitter argument. Shy, inarticulate men found words— became practiced debaters. More ready speakers developed into fiery orators. Long before the day appointed the delegates began to set out from home—giving themselves more or less time according to the distance from Richmond. Spring rains had made the roads deep in mud in many places, and sometimes swollen streams which had to be forded. The difficulties may be imagined from the diary of a traveler, by stage, in Virginia at about this time, whom it took from eight in the morning till eleven at night to cover the fifty-odd miles from Williamsburg to Richmond, after a rain. Most of those from a distance went by horse-back. Patrick Henry, in his red wig and spectacles and with a stoop which made him appear elderly at fifty-eight, arrived in a gig, and Edmund Pendleton, venerable and a cripple, in a phaeton. There were a hundred and seventy delegates, and planters from far and near crowded into town to witness the battle of intellects. And there were lobbyists from distant states. Gouveneur Morris from New York was there with his family, and Robert Morris from Philadelphia—to use all the persuasion they possessed to make Virginia ratify—and, among those opposed to ratification, Oswold of the *Independent Gazetteer,* of Philadelphia. The Jockey Club, in session, gave Richmond a festive air. If Doctor Schoepf likened it to an Arabian village when only the Assembly was in session what would he have said of it in those Convention days?

In every kitchen in the town and its neighborhood, public and private, negro cooks under supervision of mistresses beaming with hospitality had been busy for days preparing for the visitation of human locusts about to descend upon the little city. Trees and grass wore their liveliest green. Roses were in bloom, strawberries ripe, and bird music mingled with the pleasant roar of which all diaries and letters of the day make note, of the leaping Falls of James River.

Edmund Pendleton, a friend of the Constitution, leaning on his crutches, but vigorous of intellect, was unanimously elected President of the Convention. George Wythe, like minded, was made chairman of the Committee of the whole—a little man of ripe years, but erect and keen-eyed, with thin, clear-cut features and a dome-like pate, bald, except at the rear where a row of crisp little grey curls appeared above his white stock. The giants in debate were about evenly divided for and against ratification, and were arrayed against one another in the presence of a breathless audience which included the town merchants, who shut up shop in order to be present. In favor of the Constitution was Governor Edmund Randolph—handsome, charming, and adored by the people. He had declined to sign it in Philadelphia and sprung a sensation when he announced a change of mind. And George Nicholas—able lawyer, gallant soldier, strong of family connection, but short, thick, fat, with bald head, grey eyes set beneath bushy eyebrows and a big beak of a nose. Big of brain and of body, he was in debate cold and clear of voice, and powerful. Striking in contrast, physically, was that great captain of advocates of the Constitution, James Madison—a small man with a smaller voice, and exquisite in dress with his blue and buff clothes and immaculate ruffled shirt and wrist-bands, and his hair powdered on top and queued and tied with ribbon at the back. Another contrast was provided by beautiful, dashing, clarion-voiced Light Horse Harry Lee and John Marshall—far weightier in debate and equally magnetic in an entirely different style. He was gaunt, dark, tousle-haired, but perfectly at ease in an ill-fitting summer coat bought for the occasion for a dollar.

Among those opposed to the Constitution were Patrick Henry of the wizard words, and George Mason, snowy-haired and dark-eyed, impressively attired in black silk, coming in together—arm-in-arm—from the new Swan Tavern on Broad and Tenth Streets, three blocks from the Academy; James Monroe—young, awkward in speech and manner; Benjamin Harrison, of " Berkeley ", an old aristocrat of towering figure, " elegantly arrayed in a rich suit of blue and buff, a long queue tied with a black ribbon dangling from his full locks of snow, and his long black boots encroaching on his knees ", and William Grayson, brilliant and witty. Two great Virginians who would have been arrayed on opposite sides were absent. Jefferson, who was against ratification, was in Paris, occupied with his duties as Minister to France, and Washington, in retirement at Mount Vernon waiting, watching and hoping. How he would have enjoyed a wireless apparatus!

The battle of wits lasted for three long weeks and then, on June 25th, arose the gigantic form of James Innes. He had been chosen to close the debate for ratification and is said to have spoken " like one inspired." Scholarly John Tyler delivered the parting shaft for the opposition. The vote was taken and victory for the Constitution by a beggarly margin of eight votes announced. " And so ", in the words of Senator Beveridge, " closed the greatest debate ever held over the Constitution and one of the ablest parliamentary debates of history."

Patrick Henry, accustomed to carrying everything before him, and others as passionately convinced as he that national government would be a death blow to hardly won freedom, went sadly away to their homes.

Early in the next year the Virginia electors met in the Capitol to do their part in making the great Washington the first President of the United States. On March 26, 1791, Richmond was honored and delighted by a visit from the adored soldier as head of the nation.

PART III

A NEW ERA

(1790—1800)

CHAPTER VIII

THE CAPITOL

WHEN Jefferson was abroad as Minister to France he fell in love—but not with a woman. From " Nismes ", he wrote to a friend in Richmond: " Here I am gazing whole hours at the Maison Quarrée, like a lover at his mistress."

Appealed to, in 1785, for a design for Virginia's capitol building, he immediately saw not only " a favorable opportunity to introduce into the state an example of architecture in the classic style of antiquity ", but to crown Richmond's Capitol Hill with a reproduction of the " antient " Roman temple on Gallic soil which had captivated the artist and dreamer in him. He had a small plaster model made of it —using Ionic columns because of the difficulty of reproducing the Corinthian and " drew a plan for the interior with apartments necessary for legislative, executive and judiciary purposes." Largely through Marshall's efforts the little Masonic Hall on East Franklin Street (the oldest in America), had been built in this year, and the cornerstone of the Capitol was laid with solemn ritual in the following, but not until the fall of 1788 did the Assembly meet in it. Even then, its thick brick walls were bare of their coat of grey stucco which, with other finishing touches, it soon received—Richmond people contributing liberally to defray the cost. The white marble figure which dominates the rotunda is the only statue of Washington done from life and is a jewel of which Virginia has always been proud. Its sculptor—the great Houdon—was selected by Jefferson and sent from Paris to Mount Vernon, where he made a long visit, studying, measuring and modelling his illustrious subject, while work on the capitol building was in progress at Richmond. One of the niches in the wall of the rotunda holds a bust of Lafayette, also by Houdon.

Not satisfied with only an indoor effigy of Washington for the Capitol, books were opened by a committee, with John Marshall as chairman, to raise subscriptions for a monument in the Square. Various interruptions made the work lag, and not until Washington's Birthday 1858, when Richmond's population had grown to over 35,000, was the equestrian statue made by Thomas Crawford (at the cost of $100,000), unveiled. It was cast in Munich and shipped from Amsterdam, and lazy winds took the same length of time to bring it to Richmond that Columbus spent in crossing the Atlantic three and a half centuries earlier. Richmond turned out to watch the unloading. The long ropes attached to the truck on which the box, weighing eighteen tons, was placed became human ropes, as all the men and boys in town rushed to them and, cheering and being cheered, hauled the statue through the streets to Capitol—a performance which was repeated thirty years later when the Lee statue was hauled through the city to its pedestal by cheering boys and men. The Governor and Mayor made speeches from atop the great box which held the bronze Washington. The artillery saluted. When the eagerly awaited twenty-second arrived, and the veil was drawn, there stood revealed not only a life-like Washington on a life-like charger, with some of the heroes who had been his friends and associates forming a ring of bronze giants below and around him, but a work of art which has grown in fame with the years. In fame and in beauty, for the group is now mantled with the pale-green, moss-like mold which is time's gift to fine bronze. For the features and proportions of Washington, Crawford followed Houdon. The standing figures are Henry, Jefferson, Marshall, Nelson, Mason and Lewis. Crawford died before modelling all of them and the missing statues were added later by Randolph Rogers.

After the unveiling there was a round of entertaining for the distinguished guests who had come from every part of the country—many states being represented by governor and staff in full regalia. The gala day was followed by a merry night. There were fireworks, illuminated arches and transparencies. At the taverns—now proudly called hotels—there were balls. Edwin Booth was playing Shakespeare at the theatre and there was plenty of time to see him and take in a ball afterward, if one liked. Skies frowned, winds sighed, streets were muddy rivulets, but save in a house here and there whose dim-lit silence was the sign of illness or death, the people ate and drank, laughed and chatted and (when floors had been cleared), danced. The stately minuet had gone out of fashion but the newly imported waltz alternated with quadrilles and the lancers, for which darkies with beaming, dreaming faces scraped their fiddles and called the figures. And of course, the evening ended with the rollicking Virginia reel.

Long before the Washington Monument was placed Capitol Square had been changed from a crude, rugged area to a green isle in a sea of town activities. Its hills and dales were clothed with turf and shaded with trees, and walks were laid out. The year 1810 had seen the Governor's Mansion built and 1824 the brick Bell Tower succeeded the frame one on the same site. The tower bell was for generations the tocsin of Richmond—pealing for joyful events, tolling for funerals, and warning of fires and other alarms. In the wars of 1812 and 1861-5, it rang to rally the regular and volunteer soldiers to defend the city against expected attacks. In 1865, its bell was cracked and was removed. It has never been replaced, but the voiceless tower still stands in its corner of the Square exciting the curiosity of passers-by and giving the old-world scene an added touch of quaintness. As time went on other statues were added. One of Henry Clay—erected by the "Whig ladies" of Virginia; one of Stonewall Jackson—the gift of some admirers in England; one of Governor William Smith; one of Doctor Hunter McGuire—Richmond's great physician. The remarkable taste displayed in placing the buildings and statuary in the Square, which covers six city blocks, is an adornment in itself. The Capitol, the Governor's Mansion (with its embowering trees) and the Washington group each occupies the exact spot where it is most effective. South of them the hill falls away abruptly, giving this Richmond forum an impressive elevation, and seen from afar, before skyscrapers of neighboring streets began to stand in their light, the classic form and delicate columns of the Capitol, rising above a city of village-like air whose crudities kindly distance softened, made a charming picture. This modest memorial of "the grandeur that was Rome" was doubtless an influence in the development of beauty-worship in Poe's poetic soul, for in childhood the Capitol was a short walk from his home in one direction, and from Shockoe Creek where he learned to swim in another, and immediately opposite was the home of his chum Robert Stanard, whose sympathetic mother inspired the poem beginning: "Helen, thy beauty is to me." Later he lived in full view of it with his child-bride and he and she must have often walked together under the trees in the Square. The *Southern Literary Messenger* building, where the foundations of his fame were laid, was just a little way down town from it, and the inn at which he oftenest made

RICHMOND FROM THE CANAL BANK, 1833
From an old engraving

RICHMOND IN 1853, LOOKING WEST FROM CHURCH HILL
From an old engraving

himself at home was at the sign of " The Swan " just around the corner. The Capitol was long the very heart of the city—both literally and figuratively. In pleasant weather its " square " was a favorite place to stroll and chat in, its benches to rest upon. Children and their " Mammies " swarmed there to see and feed the squirrels. The Governor's house has always been a place of democratic hospitality—especially during sessions of the Assembly. Then in the early times, a bowl of toddy stood on the sideboard every day for members who chose to drop in to partake of as they pleased.

But most of all the Capitol itself has been, in a broad sense, a community centre. It was the Capitol of the state when many of those who helped to make Virginia famous as the mother of great men were babes at her breast. During the Civil War it was the Capitol of the Confederate States as well as the Capitol of Virginia. But it has not only provided a stage for enactment of scenes which have become an important part of the history of Virginia and America, its chambers have provided gathering places for social, literary, patriotic and public-welfare groups. After over a century of service want of more room necessitated enlargement, and wings were thrown out from its north and south walls. While these have lessened the resemblance to the Maison Carrée, they have been harmoniously designed, with pillars, pilasters and cornices like those of the main building.

In earlier days Capitol Square had been filled with ruts and gullies and crossed by a road used as a short cut between Broad and Main Streets. Until about 1800, Broad Street ended at First Street. Lower down were Academy Square (with its theatre which was succeeded by Monumental Church), Swan Tavern, and a few other scattered houses, and at its western extremity two merchants, Bootright and Garthwright, on opposite corners, were friendly rivals in trade. At their stores the long, canvas-covered four or six horse wagons bringing produce down from the Blue Ridge Mountains made a first stop as they emerged from Brook Road into the city. After supplying the enterprising merchants named with flour, butter, hemp, wax, tallow, flaxseed, feathers, deer and bearskins, furs, ginseng, snake-root and so on, they creaked on to Governor Street across whose deep gullies they made a difficult passage to Main Street, to dispose of the remainder of their cargo to merchants there, around whose stores —it is written—" The fleets of wagons that would assemble in brisk times looked like the baggage train of a small army." Or perhaps the descent was made through the gully-furrowed road across Capitol Square. Among unique wares brought in by these overland ships noted by the author of *Richmond in By-Gone Days,* was a bunch of dried rattlesnakes " to make viper broth for consumptive patients." Those early mountaineers were as clever in concealing money from possible robbers as some of their successors are in disguising " moonshine." A perfectly innocent looking bale of hemp or cask of wax or tallow might be found, on investigation, to contain a bag of gold or silver coin.

CHAPTER IX

ENTER THE TWO PARSONS

THE Capitol has served both Church and State. We have seen a political convention assembled in St. John's, let us see the congregation of St. John's on its knees in the Hall of the House of Delegates. Richmond early showed a tendency to grow westward, away from the church on the hill, instead of eastward, toward it. The answer is easy. The city said to have been built like Rome, on seven hills, really covered two principal heights, divided by the deep valley through which coursed Shockoe Creek. These were subdivided by ravines known as " gullies." Church Hill is steep, Shockoe is gradual. Settlement, following the line of least resistance, spread over Shockoe Hill and long neglected the neighborhood of St. John's. To tell the whole truth, there was a spiritual Hill of Difficulties between the church and a large part of the people as steep as that of clay and gravel. Since the Revolution the Church of England, like everything else English, had fallen into disfavor. Enthusiasm for the French Revolution and the influence of the writings of Paine, Godwin, Rousseau and Voltaire were widespread in Virginia, as elsewhere in America, and for a time in Richmond, now aptly called " The City of Churches ", atheism was rife, church-going unpopular, especially with the element most warmly attached to Jefferson. Anyone depressed over imagined falling off in church-going since those good old days is borrowing trouble. A handful of Methodists met in the old Capitol and in the Courthouse, until neighbors complained of being disturbed by their vociferous style of worship and they had to make a stable near Old Market serve as a place for a joyful noise until their church on Franklin and Nineteenth Streets was opened, with twenty-eight white and twenty-two colored members. In 1780, the Baptists made a beginning toward organizing a congregation, with fourteen members. In 1810 their evangelist, John Courtney, was preaching to a small group in a frame house and after a while they built a brick "meeting house", on Broad Street, two squares below the site of the present First Baptist Church building—with its huge membership whose automobiles fill the streets around it whenever its doors are open. There were Quakers in Richmond from very early times. In *Richmond in By-Gone Days* Samuel Mordecai gives a pen-picture of one of them (Mr. Lowndes), and says that many such figures had formerly been seen in the streets. He was "a fine type of the Quaker in personal appearance and in dress—with his broad-brimmed hat, drab suit, the coat of plainest cut without a superfluous button, waistcoat in same style, both of ample length and breadth, knee breeches, gray stockings, and silver knee- and shoe-buckles." His house (on top of a steep hill), and his "falling gardens", could be seen from the rear windows of Bowler's Tavern.

In a tiny house near Mayo's Bridge lived the good and scholarly priest, Abbé Du Bois, who ministered to the spiritual needs of a little band of Roman Catholics. But with the people in general, church-going was at a low ebb.

The "Two Parsons" changed all that. One of them, the Reverend John Buchanan, rector of St. John's, decided to bring Mahomet to the mountain. If the people would not come up the hill to the preacher he would go down the hill to the people and give them a service in the new Capitol every other Sunday. On alternate Sundays his chum, the Reverend John D. Blair, gave a Presbyterian service there

72

to practically the same congregation, and later on preached at St. John's on the Sundays when Doctor Buchanan was at the Capitol. The choir (which sat in the gallery), was composed of " the sweet and harmonious voices of some of Richmond's favorite female vocalists ", with the tenor of " Nekervis " and the " mellow, deep-toned bass voices of old Blagrove and Southgate—men of character and note." Among the instruments which accompanied them were " Lynch's soul-inspiring flute " and " Fitzwilson's huge bass viol, in front of which he could scarcely bring his arms to wield his immense bow on account of the rotundity of his person." Parson Buchanan had a beautiful voice to which a slight Scotch accent lent charm in speaking or in reading the Prayer Book Service.

The two Parsons loved not only each other but everybody in Richmond, of every age, class, color and condition. Their religion was sincere and their scholarship genuine, but their black coats made them none the less human and, at proper times, they could play as ardently as they could preach—for they also, were but grown-up boys. They were at home in all companies and without thought of offense or of causing a brother to offend, they enjoyed (as did many another devout parson of the time), a good dinner, a rubber of whist, a game of quoits or a glass of punch. Like wise men of the proverb, they relished " a little nonsense ", and were inveterate punsters. They punned in plain English, in Scotch dialect and in negro dialect. They even punned in Latin and in French— with each other and with the learned lawyers who gave distinction to Richmond society. Their benevolent acts and their humorous sayings and doings made them idols of the people and rendered their influence immense in their time, and they are among the happiest traditions of the old city today. They literally fill a book, for, fortunately, Mr.

George Wythe Munford who was only a boy when they were old men, but in whose home they were intimate, has kept them alive in his quaint and now rare volume, *The Two Parsons*. Parson Buchanan was a confirmed old bachelor, but devoted to children, especially those of Parson Blair. See him as he passes along the street or under the trees in Capitol Square—hands clasped behind him. He wears a broad-brimmed hat and a wide-skirted black coat down to his knees, a high stock, knickerbockers and long stockings, silver knee-buckles and shoe-buckles. His big pockets contain confections, in case he should meet little folk. Parson Blair, strolling beside him, is tall and spare with a countenance whose gravity in repose gives no hint of what a jolly good fellow he is. His black dress is more modern than his friend's and he carries a stick. These two meet almost daily, but that does not check the flow between them of little notes in rhyme and in prose. Here is a sample:

"Ad Reverendissime Johannem Buchanan.
Dear Brother:—I received today as a marriage fee, an elegant turkey. You are so obstinate that you will not take unto yourself a rib. I know you cannot eat a whole turkey by yourself—come and eat it with me, and I will help you to a 'side bone' or a 'hug me close,' and this perhaps will remind you of your duty.
Affectionately, J. D. B."

Parson Buchanan, like many other Richmond gentlemen, had a farm near town—on the site of the earlier Bacon's Quarter, on which now stands the R. F. and P. freight depot. Buchanan's Spring, in a grove of old oaks, was a spot around which centred much recreational life. It was Richmond's country club of the day. The Barbecue Club met there on pleasant Saturday afternoons and, in summer, the Two Parsons—its only honorary members—pitched quoits there, with John Marshall and other grown-up boys, as regularly as they preached in St. John's and the Capitol on Sundays. It was the resort of the volunteer military companies on festive occasions. Military service was encouraged in Virginia, for though the State had played so important a part in bringing about ratification of the United States Constitution, the Republican party, with Jefferson as its leader (which later became the Democratic party), was still uneasy lest the new government should become a new tyrant. It was watching every move of the Federalists and quietly putting the State in position to defend herself with arms, in case of inroads on her rights. In 1794, an Armory capable of equipping 100,000 men on short notice was erected between the canal and the river. Its central building boasted a cupola and was flanked by commodious wings, and its parade ground was brave with long rows of cannon and pyramids of balls. The Richmond Light Infantry Blues —the first company of volunteers to organize—found it difficult to complete their ranks because their uniforms were too suggestive of British Red Coats; so they turned out in dark blue with white facings and black stocks, with long black plumes tipped with white floating from tall black leather helmets—a uniform which with slight change, makes a gallant show today and has brought the Blues thunderous applause in many a parade. They took the town by storm and their ranks were quickly filled by the élite. Almost as dashing was the Independent Volunteer Company of Infantry—in their long blue coats faced with red, their white vests, breeches and stockings, their black stocks, knee-bands and spatterdashes, their jaunty cocked hats set off with black feathers tipped with red, and the cockade of the United States. Later on other companies were formed, and during the war-scare of 1807, there was a home-guard appropriately named the " Silver Greys ", composed of men too old for military duty.

Let us see the Two Parsons making holiday with the soldier boys. It is a Fourth of July and the Blues are to have a great dinner at Buchanan Spring. The Parsons are invited and Captain Murphy calls for them in a carriage which is escorted by the company, marching in quick time to the place of rendezvous. Arrived there, they stack arms and line up, single file, while the Captain in his gay regalia, with a black-coated parson on each arm, passes down the line that the reverend guests of honor may shake hands with each of their hosts. Pretty sight, is it not? The Captain makes one more introduction—to the Blues' famous blue bowl, which is of India china and holds thirty-two gallons. It stands on a table near the spring, in the custody of Jasper Crouch, a negro pastmaster in mixing contents for such a vessel. After filling it with ice to one-third of its capacity, Jasper adds a mixture composed of four parts of old Cognac brandy to one part of Jamaica rum, " a dash of old Murdock Madeira ", some fresh lemons and sugar " to taste." Captain Murphy warns him that the Parsons "touch lightly" and must have something delicate. The Master of the Bowl dips each of them a glass, saying : " Mars' Blair, you is a judge, is de 'roma de proper flavor? " and " Mars' Buchanan, *you* knows what's good, what *you* say? "

" Couldn't be beat, Jasper," exclaim both, in unison.

Soon dinner is served. It has been prepared by the first of two dusky John Dabneys, as fine artists in their line as Jasper Crouch is in his —and as much a part of the history of Richmond. The Parsons are seated on the right and left of the Captain. The popping of Champagne bottles is the signal for the Captain to rise. Ordering, " charge your glasses! " he gives the first toast: " The Reverend

ENTER THE TWO PARSONS

John D. Blair and the Reverend John Buchanan recruiting officers for a holy army. The bounty they offer for devoted service is a blissful future without money and without price." (Applause and calls for Parson Blair). He, rising, responds: "Gentlemen of the Blues, I glory in being a ' recruiting officer for a holy army.' The emblem of our flag is peace. In the language of the heavenly host at the birth of our Master I give you Peace. ' Glory to God in the highest, and on earth peace, good will toward men.' And in the language of the Master Himself, I will say to the tempestuous waves of strife and sin, ' Peace, be still '." (Cheers and calls for Parson Buchanan). He, standing, and smiling down the long table into bright, eager faces, says, in his musical Scotch tones: "Blues, you know the perfect accord that exists between Brother Blair and myself, and yet on this occasion we are apparently sundered. He's for Peace, I'm for War. Yes, I give you War! Uncompromising War against the Devil and his hosts of iniquity!" (More cheers and a few bugle notes say Amen to this). Other toasts follow and the dinner goes merrily to its end, when up canters Colonel Robert Gamble (of Gamble's Hill), at the head of a troop of cavalry which has celebrated the day at Goddin's Spring. The Governor rides beside him and the black bugler, old Fredrick, picturesquely heads the column, playing "Washington's March." The newcomers are heartily welcomed. They help the Blues to empty their big bowl, then all return to town. The companies march to the Capitol Square where they fire their evening salute, and so comes "the end of a perfect day."

CHAPTER X

UNDERCURRENTS

AND now for another side of the picture. Richmond was prospering. The population had grown to more than 5,000 souls. Substantial homes were increasing. Among them was the sturdy John Marshall house, which gave Marshall Street its name. The Bank of Richmond, which gave Bank Street (bounding Capitol Square on the south) its name, had been incorporated, by leading citizens (including Marshall) — with its unique provision that whoever should offer it fraudulent money should " suffer death without benefit of clergy." The Mutual Assurance Association had opened in a yellow building near the Capitol, a few blocks from its present sky-scraper. Colonel John Mayo had spanned James River and connected Richmond with Manchester by a predecessor of the present stately Mayo's Bridge. The James River Canal had been built (during Washington's presidency) around The Falls, and furnished a means of bringing produce— including tobacco, upon which much of Richmond's present wealth was founded and still depends—down to market from the upper country. Later, when the canal was finished, it afforded a new means of travel which was long a picturesque feature of social life.

The Penitentiary—suggested by Jefferson as a step toward prison reform—had been designed by the Baltimore architect, Latrobe, and was under way. Hitherto, from jail to gallows had been the rule with criminals convicted of serious offenses in Virginia, as in many other states. The Square on Franklin Street between First and Second

THE HOME OF JOHN MARSHALL
John Marshall High School in the rear

DINING-ROOM IN JOHN MARSHALL HOUSE
By Courtesy of the Association for the Preservation of Virginia Antiquities

UNDERCURRENTS

Streets, later occupied by Linden Row, was first bought for the Penitentiary, but Colonel Thomas Rutherfoord, disturbed at the prospect of such a neighbor, arranged an exchange of the property for the present site of the State prison, and saved Richmond's finest residential street.

In depicting scenes of the thriving town with its young-hearted people whose joy of living and satisfaction with themselves and one another were unspoiled by sophistication or ennui, and among whom the genial Two Parsons went about doing good, it would be easy to confine one's brush to rose-colored pigments—but the story would be only half true. In lives of persons, cities, and nations there are often undercurrents of which the outward aspect gives no hint until something causes an explosion which brings them violently to the surface. In Richmond one such undercurrent was party strife. In the spring of 1798, Congress passed the Alien Act empowering the President to order out of the country " any foreigner whom he might believe to be dangerous to the peace and safety of the United States," and the " Sedition Act," making it a crime to " write, utter or publish " any " false, scandalous and malicious writing against Congress and the President "—an act regarded as an attempt of the government to destroy freedom of the press. These acts caused a tempest of hostility throughout the Union which nowhere raged more fiercely than in Virginia's capital. They made the fear that the new government might exceed its powers a fact in many minds, and crystallized political opinion into two bitterly antagonistic parties which broke up friendships, divided families and inaugurated a carnival of mud-slinging.

The Assembly met in the new Capitol on December 21, 1798, and, in a stormy session, passed resolutions declaring loyalty to the Union and the Constitution but most emphatically protesting against the objectionable Acts. The majority of the Assembly's members, and of the people of Virginia whom they represented, were sympathizers with the French Revolution and devoted to Jefferson's party, notwithstanding that Washington and Marshall were on the other side and that even Patrick Henry, who had so eloquently opposed the Constitution, had been won over by Washington. The resolutions caused intense excitement and bitter discussion throughout the United States. Party feeling rose higher and higher. Federalists and Republicans would not patronize the same taverns or walk on the same side of the street. Even such great men as Jefferson and Marshall developed a scorn of each other which lasted the rest of their lives. Jefferson expressed fear that the Federalists might create a monarchy by making Adams president for life and then fixing the succession in his family. When Monroe, who had become a strong Republican, was elected Governor, *The Virginia Federalist* (published in Richmond), declared the day to be one of "mourning" and announced: "Virginia's misfortune may be comprised in one short sentence—Monroe is elected." Republicans decorated themselves with the French tricolor as a badge of their party and increased the disgust of their opponents. A foul-mouthed, foul-minded creature by the name of John Thompson Callender—a Scotchman who had been obliged to fly his own country for political offenses—drifted to Richmond, and the Republicans unable to resist using his facility for calling names they were ashamed to call themselves, permitted his abusive articles to disgrace their organ—*The Examiner*. He was tried for libelling the President, found guilty and sent to jail—but continued to write his letters, which continued to appear in *The Examiner*, dated "Richmond Jail." He also brought out while there a volume of his book *The Prospect Before Us*—aided, it was said, by a gift of a hundred dollars from Jefferson. Yet Jefferson, himself, on becoming President, furnished a new target for his darts. It is not surprising that so much bad feeling should have resulted in several duels, though it seems strange that in one of them the challenging party should have borne the name of William Penn—who slightly wounded his adversary, Colonel John Mayo.

Bitter as the feeling was, there were sometimes tilts in jocular vein. The Two Parsons, though Federalists, kept out of active politics. One day they went " arm in arm " to dine with Mr. Munford's father, who was a Republican—or Democrat, which paradoxical as it sounds was then the same thing. Parson Blair's terrier went along and no sooner had the party arrived than the dog was pounced upon by the Munford cat, which had to be taken from the room in order to restore peace.

" I know," said Parson Blair, "*that* cat is a Democrat!"

" To be sure she is," said Mr. Munford " and she has had instinct enough to know that Towser was a Federalist. She couldn't stand that! "

Of course college students were fiery partisans. Those of William and Mary, many of whom were Richmond boys, debated as to whether or not they should wear mourning for Washington's death, on December 14, 1799. A majority, though not all, voted for it. In Richmond all parties forgot petty quarrels and sorrowed together for the great chieftain. Marshall made an oration at the Capitol, Christmas gaieties were omitted and citizens went about in crêpe sleeve-bands for thirty days.

And now another undercurrent comes suddenly to the top and unites all factions in measures for preservation of life and property. As Buchanan's Spring provided a primitive country club for white folk, so Young's Spring and the banks of the brook north of town which gave Brook Road and " Brook Hill " (the Stewart estate) their names, were out-door gathering places for colored folk. There they assembled on Sundays for " preachments ", barbacues, fishing, fish-fries, quoit-pitching and so on. To passers-by, hearing their musical chanting of spiritual songs, their care-free chatter and laughter, and witnessing their merry antics, they seemed the embodiment of content and harmlessness, but now and then there were indications to the contrary. As early as 1793, a letter from an itinerant negro preacher of Richmond, suggesting an insurrection, was picked up in a Yorktown street, and one night in the same year, Mr. John Randolph heard some talk under his window which boded trouble. Nothing came of these mutterings, but as time went on signs that vague echoes of the French Revolution and of the insurrection at Haiti and San Domingo had reached Virginia negroes, and impressed them, caused uneasiness.

On Saturday, August 30, 1800, Mrs. Elizabeth Sheppard's servant, Tom, told Mr. Mosby Sheppard, with great agitation, of a plot for an uprising and massacre of white people that night, and that Mr. William Mosby of The Brook neighborhood was one of three men picked out to be the first killed. Mr. Sheppard informed Mr. Mosby and they went at once to the Governor and Mayor, who arranged to have a troop of cavalry and as many volunteers as could be raised meet near The Brook after dark, and patrol the road. A terrific storm kept both whites and blacks indoors, and doubtless the negroes heard in the thunder-claps the voice of a wrathful Jehovah, and saw in the lightning flashes of His anger. On Sunday, however, the clouds had rolled away, and one of William Mosby's servant women informed him that the plot was to be caried out that night. The town was panic-stricken.

The militia was increased and, guided by a list of names given by the widow Sheppard's Tom and her son Philip Sheppard's Pharoah, many suspects were captured and placed in the jail and penitentiary. When they were tried depositions of their own race laid bare the whole ghastly plot. "General" Gabriel, as the chief plotter called himself was captured on a schooner in Norfolk Harbour, and he and other ring-leaders were publicly hanged. Some of the others were acquitted; some pardoned. Governor Monroe rewarded Tom and Pharoah with their freedom—paying the Sheppards five hundred dollars apiece from the state treasury for the loss of such faithful servants.

"General" Gabriel was the slave of Mr. Thomas Prosser of Brook Road. His plan, to carry out which he and others had been enlisting recruits at the Sunday gatherings, was made near Prosser's blacksmith shop, in the woods and his brother Solomon, the smith, reversing the order of prophecy, beat many scythes into swords—a scythe making two sword-blades. These and anything else resembling weapons they could lay hands on, were to be given the "soldiers" until they captured the arms at the Capitol and Penitentiary. A party of fifty was to set fire to the houses in Rocketts, at the east end of town. Of course the citizens would run from every direction to put the fire out, and Gabriel's army of 5000 negroes recruited from Richmond and plantations in neighboring counties, would rush on the unprotected homes and public buildings. They were ordered to attack first the Capitol, the Penitentiary, the Armory, the Governor's Mansion and the Governor's person. One of the ring-leaders, named John, who worked at the Penitentiary, promised (with the aid of recruits secured there), to kill the guards and seize the arms stored in the prison; another, Jupiter, to let the "soldiers" into the Capitol by obtaining the key from its keeper, so that the arms there could be taken. Another engaged to " enlist the warehouse boys " and another suggested collecting enough negroes to fill Capitol Square and drive all of the white people into the river. One too old to fight was made happy when employed to mould bullets. There were to be both horse and foot soldiers but almost everyone's chief ambition (as brought out in the evidence) was to be a captain, mounted on his dead master's horse and kill as many white people as possible. Mr. Prosser's man, Will, was to kill his master and have his sorrel horse, but was not made a captain because he was undersized. Mr. Young's Albert agreed to be a captain but said someone under him would have to kill his master and mistress. He could not do it because they had " raised " him. According to one witness, Isham and George were at a Sunday barbecue where fishing below The Brook bridge and quoit pitching were going on. Asked by Gabriel to join his army, each shaking the other by the hand exclaimed: " Here are our hands and hearts, we will wade to our knees in blood sooner than fail in the attempt." On the other hand, Mr. Gregory's Martin had been heard to " curse the black people for the plot." Solomon testified that all the people of Richmond were to be massacred save those who begged for quarter or agreed to join the movement. All blacks who refused to join were to be killed. Another witness said that Frenchmen (who they hoped would help them), Quakers, Methodists and poor old women who had no slaves were to be spared. Gabriel was quoted as having declared that he would save Mrs. David Meade Randolph and make her his queen because she knew so much about cooking. Mrs. Randolph was a noted housekeeper and author of a popular cookery book.

UNDERCURRENTS

" General " Gabriel's plan was (if his plot succeeded) to give all the homes of the dead Richmonders to negroes, fortify the town, and then carry his warfare throughout the state and beyond it. Though his plot failed, the dread undercurrent that it bore witness to caused uneasiness long afterward. Two years later night watches were appointed for each ward, and to any that lay awake shuddering at thought of dangers that might be lurking in the dark streets, their chant: " Oyez, Oyez, twelve o'clock and all's well " (or one, two or three o'clock, and so on), brought a comfortable sense of security.

PART IV
GROWTH AND DEVELOPMENT
(1800—1820)

CHAPTER XI

JOHN MARSHALL AND HIS CIRCLE

RICHMOND rejoiced over the election of Jefferson as President and his inauguration on March 4, 1801, was celebrated by a great public dinner in the Capitol which he had designed. Monroe, who as Governor of Virginia was living in the barnlike " palace " soon to be superseded by the present " mansion ", responded to a toast. One of the last official acts of President Adams had been the appointment of John Marshall as Chief Justice of the United States, so Virginia had the satisfaction of seeing two of her own promoted at once to the seats of the mighty. Political views of the two were so opposed that we may be sure Gossip pricked up her ears and moistened her lips in expectation of interesting clashes.

To take a glance backward, Richmond owed having John Marshall as a citizen to a girl. When he was a young veteran of the Revolution studying law at William and Mary, he met the daughters of Jacqueline Ambler, of Yorktown, at a ball and fell in love at once and forever with Mary (or Polly, as he called her), aged fourteen. Pages of his college note-book are scribbled over with her name bracketed with his—which shows the way his wits were wandering when they should have been concentrated on the learned Chancellor Wythe's lectures, and is encouraging evidence that boys cannot escape being boys, no matter how liberally Nature may have endowed them with brains or how parents and teachers may plot to circumvent them. When Richmond became Virginia's Capital and Mr. Ambler, as State Treasurer, went there to live,

Marshall abandoned his plan of settling down in his native Fauquier County, as a country lawyer, and with the same ardor and constancy which had characterized the gift of his heart to Polly Ambler, he gave himself as citizen and servant to the city which had become her home.

He and Polly did not wait to accumulate a competency. He had his profession and secured a license to practise it in Richmond—Jefferson, who was then governor, signing it on January 3, 1787. They had their love, the hopefulness of youth, and the will to wait for what they could not afford. John was a long-legged, broad-shouldered, loose-jointed young fellow of twenty-seven, with a supreme indifference as to the cut of his clothes or whether the long hair under his cocked hat was properly curled and queued, but with fine, strong features, luminous brown eyes which could be tender or merry or piercing as occasion demanded, and a personality radiating magnetism. Polly was a frail, demure girl of seventeen, adoring and being adored by this John, when they began the new year and their new life of love in a cottage, tiny and plain. After the minister's fee had been paid John cheerfully announced that he had only "one guinea left." But he and Polly did not have to bother about tomorrow's dinner, as, of course, a round of entertaining followed the wedding. He was a member of the Assembly (then in session), and had his little salary, and fees soon came in fast enough for him to live generously, not to say recklessly. For this great and good citizen was a man of the merry time he lived in.

John Marshall's day began, like that of other Richmond gentlemen, with an early walk to market—basket on arm. It was a sociable practice, rendered more so by the hospitable coffee-pot of Mr. Darmstadt—a popular Market Square merchant—around which good morning greetings were exchanged and bits of news and opinion

"UNCLE HENRY", AN EARLY RICHMOND FAMILY COACHMAN

SY GILLIAT PLAYING FOR CHILDREN TO DANCE IN A RICHMOND GARDEN
From an old painting
Photographed for the first time especially for Mrs. Stanard

were gathered up by John and taken home to Polly along with the provender, which sometimes included a live turkey carried in his free hand. And see him on a spring day, swinging along, bareheaded, with his cocked hat filled with cherries, which he is eating with boyish relish and freedom from consciousness of observation or comment. In the year of his marriage and following years, he frankly and indiscriminately entered into his account book prices of fuel, food and other housekeeping needs, of tickets to the theatre, subscriptions to dances, the Jockey Club, St. John's Church, " an Episcopal Meeting ", a " St. Taminy Society ", a corporation dinner, a barbecue, a Mason's ball, losses at whist, backgammon and the races. On a day when he spent twenty-four shillings for wood he lost eighteen pounds at whist and on another when he spent twenty-six shillings eight pence for beef he lost six pounds at backgammon. But he sometimes won, and matters were evened up. He was intimate with James Monroe—a fellow veteran of the Revolution also learning statesmanship in the Virginia Assembly. One entry reads : " Col. Monroe & self at the Play, 1-10 " and another " Pd. for Colo. Monroe £16.16. " His purse was always open and it is pleasant to know that there was enough left in it for Polly to have a fifteen dollar bonnet and a six dollar pair of silk stockings. But, indeed, the most frequent items of all are for her. " Given Polly ", " For Polly ", " sundries for Polly ", or specific items like " Gloves for Polly " are scattered over the pages.

His salary as legislator could not have gone far. During the same month (July, 1784), when the yellowed pages of his account book testify that he received for " service in the Assembly £34.4 " he " lost at whist £19 ", paid for " one quarter cask of wine £14 ", and about the same amount for expenses of birth of a child to the eighteen year old mother.

Much of the wine mentioned was doubtless used at the christening party, six weeks later. Christening parties were jolly affairs. A contemporary of John Marshall's has handed down through a grandson living in Richmond a story of one held at " Summerville ", the home of Judge William Fleming, in Chesterfield County, a few miles above The Falls. The Fleming family carriage was sent to Richmond for the minister to perform the sacred rite and the fiddler to play for the dancing afterward, and the story-teller saw it return with Parson Buchanan inside and Sy Gilliat on the box with the driver. Sy was an important member of both white and colored high society. When he and his fiddle graced formal occasions he is said to have appeared in one of the fifty court costumes of Lord Bote-tourt who had in Sy's youth been his master. See him scraping away with his bow, in embroidered silk coat, waistcoat of faded lilac, small clothes, silk stockings and big shoe-buckles. A brown wig with side curls and a long queue frames the smiling dark face, propped on the singing fiddle.

In 1788 the Marshall's moved to their new brick house at the corner of Marshall and Ninth Streets where their *ménage* was for many years an integral part of the simple home and neighborhood life that was the foundation stone upon which the distinctive character of Richmond was builded. And who were the dwellers of the mansions and simpler houses—each with its grounds and gardens—who gradually formed a neighborhood known as the " Court End " of Richmond? Few of them were built as early as John Marshall's and, with the migration across Broad Street and to the West End, most of them were later supplanted by rows of tenements; but enough of them have been saved by becoming homes of public institutions to suggest pictures of the rest.

Across Ninth Street from the Marshalls, in what is now a Roman Catholic brotherhood house, lived Alexander McRae, and on the same square Benjamin Botts, whose part as one of the counsel in the Burr trial was to give his name, like that of McRae (of the prosecution), nation wide prominence, and for whom his friends prophesied a brilliant career—little dreaming that fate had written his name in the list of those doomed to perish in a burning theatre. His son, John Minor Botts, noted politician of a later generation, was one of the boys to whom the streets and yards of the " Court End " were a playground. The rooftree of Polly Marshall's father, Jacqueline Ambler, was a white frame house in a green lawn on Tenth Street. On Clay Street, near Eleventh lived her sister, Mrs. Carrington, a bundle of whose sprightly letters, which have been preserved, were published in the *Atlantic Monthly* in the eighteen-nineties. Her husband, Colonel Edward Carrington, was a distinguished officer of the Revolution, many of whose kinsfolk are helping to carry on the world's work in Richmond and elsewhere today. Opposite the Amblers, on grounds later occupied by the Baptist Woman's College, stood the home of Colonel John Harvie. His son, General Jacqueline B. Harvie, married a daughter of John Marshall and built for her the mansion at Clay and Tenth Streets remembered as the Purcell home, which long since fell to rise again as a tenement row. A house nearly opposite the Carrington's was the home first of the Lewis Burwells and later of the John Amblers.

Tom Moore, the Irish poet (whose songs were sung to every guitar and harpsichord in Richmond), writing of a visit there in 1803, says that the most agreeable and cultivated men he met were " some Whig lawyers, one of

whom, Mr. John Wickham, was fit to adorn any court."
John Wickham came to Richmond from Long Island in
the last year of the Revolution. He and his wife, whose
flowerlike beauty has been made a matter of record by the
artist, St. Memin, were intimate friends of the Marshalls,
and their home, on Clay and Eleventh Streets, was one
of Richmond's centres of hospitality. Bob, the butler and
Bob's wife the cook, contributed handsomely to its reputation. Long after Bob had been gathered to his fathers,
a white-headed man of the colored aristocracy of the time
—old family servants—was asked why he had stopped
going to church. He replied that when he could sit beside
" Marse Wickham's Bob an' Marse Marshall's Jack " he
liked to " 'tend de meetin' ", but since " 'siety " had declined
so that he could never know whom he " sot by " he was
" better off at home."

Moore was one of the many distinguished guests of
the Wickham house, which has in later times—with a
remnant of the charming old garden—been long identified
with the name Valentine. Mr. Mann S. Valentine, and
his family were its last occupants as a private home and
it is by his will that it became The Valentine Museum.
Among many interesting objects which it houses are some
of the ideal works of Edward V. Valentine, Sculptor, the
plaster model from which his famous recumbent statue
of Lee was made, and the Valentine collection of Indian
relics. On the square opposite the Wickhams lived Judge
Philip Norborne Nicholas and Dr. James McClurg. Doctor
McClurg's house became later the home of Benjamin
Watkins Leigh, who, with Robert Stanard, Chapman
Johnson and other lawyers of their time worthily filled the
shoes of those whose talents and manners had impressed
Moore. Marshall and Wickham were contemporaries of
both generations. Mr. Leigh's third wife was Julia

94

JOHN WICKHAM

MRS. JOHN WICKHAM
From the portrait by St. Memin

THE HAYES-GREEN-McCANCE HOUSE
Rear view from the garden adorned with lakelet and statuary

Wickham, daughter of the Wickham house and grand-daughter of Doctor McClurg.

The stately White House of the Confederacy (now the Confederate Museum), on Clay and Twelfth Streets is still sometimes called the Brockenbrough House by those who know that it was originally the home of Dr. John Brockenbrough, president of the Bank of Virginia, and his wife who was Gabriella Harvie, daughter of Colonel John Harvie, and sister of John Marshall's son-in-law, General Harvie. She was the widow of Thomas Randolph, of " Tuckahoe ", and her grandmother Mary Randolph, whom she and Doctor Brockenbrough adopted, was a beauty and belle of Richmond and beyond. The brilliant, though erratic John Randolph of " Roanoke ", and fair Maria Ward, the love of his life, were intimates in this house, and when their affair came to its mysterious and unhappy end it was to Mrs. Brockenbrough that the young girl entrusted her lover's letters, in a sealed packet, with the request that after her death it should be burned with its seal unbroken.

The home of Doctor Brockenbrough's brother, Judge William Brockenbrough of the Court of Appeals, was a simpler house of red brick on Broad Street, across Ninth from the Swan Tavern, and on the site of the present Smithdeal College.

Among other lawyers of the coterie admired by Moore were Governor Edmund Randolph (the site of whose house is now covered by the City Hall) ; U. S. District Attorney George Hay, whose house on Ninth Street, opposite Capitol Square, was later the home of Judge Stanard, husband of Poe's " Helen " ; Daniel Call, whose wife was another of " Polly " Marshall's sisters; William Wirt, a familiar figure in the Court End of town, though he made his home in a different neighborhood; witty Jack Baker; and caustic Jock Warden, a Scotchman with features as fascinatingly grotesque as a battered marble Satyr in an old Richmond garden. A quaint story connecting him with Wickham, Hay and Wirt has been handed down. The old Roman custom of tying hay on the horns of cattle to give warning that they were vicious gave rise to an expression *habet foenum in cornu* (has hay on his horns), to describe a dangerous person. One day when Wickham and Hay were on opposite sides in a law case, Wickham, after an argument in which he had the better of his adversary, remarked: "You may take either horn of the dilemma you choose." Mr. Warden, with a gleam of enjoyment lighting his comical face, leaned toward the equally entertained but contrastingly handsome Wirt, and whispered: *Habet foenum in cornu.* Mr. Wirt, smiling, scribbled on a piece of paper:

> "Wickham one day in open court,
> Was tossing Hay on his horns for sport;
> Jock, rich in wit and Latin too,
> Cried, *Habet foenum in cornu.*"

On Seventh Street between Clay and Leigh was the round-chimneyed, château-like house of the financier Albert Gallatin, whose marriage to Miss Allegre was one of the romances of the day. It later became the home of Dr. James D. McCaw, father of Dr. James B. McCaw, and later still passed to Mr. Conway Robinson, who built on the same lot the house long known as the Presbyterian and Methodist Home for Ladies. On Eighth and Leigh Streets was the beautiful Hayes-Green-McCance mansion and its garden, embellished not only by shrubberies and flowers but with a lakelet and statuary, some of which may be seen today in the Valentine Museum garden and in the garden of the Sculptor's studio—to which they add a touch of old-world atmosphere.

Mr. Hay's home opposite Capitol Square, and its chatelaine, the first Mrs. Hay, became conspicuous during the " loo " craze which took the feminine half of Richmond society by storm in 1805. Mrs. Hay became its most ardent votary and her home its headquarters. Gentlemen acting as escorts of the ladies of the Court End and other select neighborhoods of Richmond joined them in a preliminary " dish " of tea and occasionally in their game, but oftener enjoyed a quiet rubber of whist, while waiting into the wee sma' hours to take the fair gamblers home. They would begin with a trifling stake, but according to Mordecai, in *Richmond in Bygone Days,* " The pool would sometimes accumulate a score or two of dollars and even three or four score." He neglects to say how much would be put up at the " quiet " game of whist in the next room, but continues: " As the contents of the pool increased, so did the excitement and anxiety of the players . . . Many a charming face would lose its sweetness, many a rosy cheek its hue ; many a bright eye would almost be dimmed by a rising tear, and many an apparently smooth and gentle temper would betray the indications of an approaching storm. Gentle accents would be changed to loud tones, and endearing epithets to harsh and insulting ones. " In June, 1806, the appearance in the papers of some satirical verses signed " Hickory Cornhill ", gave a sudden check to the craze. The ladies could not stand being laughed at. During the following year Mrs. Hay's death made a quiet season for the circle in which she moved and the game of loo was heard of no more.

CHAPTER XII

THE TRIAL OF AARON BURR

AND now Richmond again becomes the theatre for a national drama, with all America as audience. Richmond and its neighborhood and visitors from all directions pack every point of vantage, while press and post broadcast each word and gesture of the actors as speedily as may be, so that, in town and country the continent over, men and women pore over their newspapers and letters, breathlessly visualizing the scenes enacted in a pillared Capitol on a green hill overlooking a tumbling river—the scenes in the trial for high treason of Aaron Burr, late Vice-President of the United States, and his accomplice in the crime of which he either is or is not guilty, Herman Blennerhassett. The man cast by Fortune for the principal part in the play is of slight physique, distinguished bearing and magnetic address. See him make his entrance with perfect poise, theatrically attired in rich black silk, pains-takingly powdered and queued. His face is a white marble mask out of which look big, black, burning eyes into the equally brilliant and searching ones of Chief Justice Marshall who is to preside over the tribunal that will decide his fate. On each side is an impressive array of legal talent. For the prosecution there are George Hay, Alexander McRae and Cæsar A. Rodney; for the defense, John Wickham, Edmund Randolph, William Wirt, Benjamin Botts, Jack Baker and Luther Martin. The quality of many of the host of witnesses is as notable as the legal talent. The indictment has been brought in by a grand jury with John Randolph of " Roanoke " as foreman. Among clever reporters from far and near is the youthful Washington Irving, representing a New York paper.

Soon after the Burr-Hamilton duel a travelling showman had brought a representation of it in wax works to Richmond. It had been exhibited at Washington Tavern, opposite Capitol Square, and seen by everybody who could raise fifty cents. Now, here was the survivor in person, on trial in the Capitol building! According to the standards of the time, Alexander Hamilton had given Aaron Burr provocation to justify settlement upon "the field of honor." Yet in challenging this brilliant and idolized statesman, and in firing the fatal shot, Burr had ended his own career. His ambition was still alive, however, and he had gone west to find fresh means of gratifying it. Was his plan merely to settle new lands or was it to divide the Union and set up an empire over which he was to reign? Who knows? Who will ever know? Whatever his intent, the scene of his planning, or plotting, was the island of the Irishman, Blennerhassett, in the Ohio River, and thus within the bounds of Virginia, so after a flight southward —in disguise—and after a dramatic capture, he was brought to Virginia's capital for trial. The well-known animosity between Judge Marshall, who was believed to have a leaning toward Burr, and President Thomas Jefferson, who hated him, added a dash of spice to the case. At a crucial point in it the Chief Justice summoned the President as a witness, but Mr. Jefferson made public service an excuse and Marshall did not press the point.

While Burr and Blennerhassett were out on bail they were wined and dined like distinguished guests. One of the most interesting figures brought to Richmond by the trial was Burr's beautiful and beloved daughter, Theodosia, and father and daughter made friends everywhere. Mr.

RICHMOND: ITS PEOPLE AND ITS STORY

Wickham was one of those who gave a dinner to his picturesque client. The Chief Justice was a guest and was
severely criticised for the breach of his usual good judgment. Blennerhassett kept a diary in which he gossips
genially of Richmond people, and of kindness he received
from them, in prison and out of it. On the evening of
August 6th, he was visited in the penitentiary by Mr.
Wickham and Mr. Botts of the Burr counsel. He writes:
" These and Mr. Randolph said all three considered themselves voluntarily engaged as my counsel, without any
expectation of pecuniary assistance from me. " Mrs.
Robert Gamble, mother-in-law of William Wirt, took
him under her wing. Her home on the Hill of the Grey
Cross was not far from the penitentiary, and she, Mrs.
Chevallie and Mrs. Edward Carrington sent delicacies to
supplement his prison fare. When the heat of the dog
days was at its height " a present of fruit and good butter
and fine calves' feet jelly was sent, in ice, by Mrs. Gamble."
When free, on bail, he " drank tea " at the Gamble Mansion
and also in what was later known as the Allan House, with
Mrs. David Meade Randolph, then its mistress. She was
the same whose fame for housewifery caused " General "
Gabriel to order that her life should be spared by his insur-
rectionists. Blennerhassett found her a woman of
" charming manners and masculine mind. " Of course,
so notable a hostess and homemaker could not have been
lacking in feminine charm, but as mentality was then
regarded as peculiarly a man's attribute, masculine was
the adjective with which to describe it.

Blennerhassett was intimate, too, at the home of Doctor
Brockenbrough—who had been a member of the grand
jury. He says: " Mrs. Brockenbrough is regarded as
the nearest approach in this town to a savante and bel
esprit." He was a frequent guest at the Harmonic Society

100

where he met—among other social favorites—beautiful Sally Conyers and heard her flutelike voice. One evening there he "took part in a symphony and a quartette by Pleyel."

The spring of 1807 had been just opening in Richmond when, on March 24th, Burr had arrived under strong guard, on the stage from the South. On September 1st, after endless examination of evidence, endless battles between counsel, endless elaborate opinions of the Chief Justice, an ambiguous verdict was brought in: "We of the jury find that Aaron Burr is not proved to be guilty under the indictment by any evidence submitted to us. We therefore find him not guilty." That is to say the prisoner was acquitted, but not cleared. His counsel tried to have the verdict changed to a simple "not guilty", but the jury was adamant. Not until seven weeks later—October 20th—did the curtain fall on the final act of the drama, when, closing the trial for the second indictment (for "misdemeanor") brought in by the grand jury, John Marshall gave his last opinion in the case. To wit: that there was sufficient evidence to commit Burr and Blennerhassett, and that they be sent to the State of Ohio where the misdemeanor was committed and there be tried, if there should be an indictment. He then bade the prisoners goodbye, turned his back on the Capitol, and "galloped to the mountains" for a period of rest at his farm. The prisoners set out on their journey to Ohio, but the government there never took up their prosecution and to the end of time the verdict will stand: Acquitted, but not cleared.

CHAPTER XIII

THE " CHESAPEAKE "-" LEOPARD " AFFAIR

In the midst of the Burr trial a new excitement arose. Strained relations with England had continued to create uneasiness, and the outrageous attack in Virginia waters, of the British frigate *Leopard* on the American frigate *Chesapeake,* a number of whose crew were killed and wounded was bitterly resented throughout the country. In Virginia's Capital a committee of citizens draughted resolutions urging the government to avenge the insult, and offering their lives and fortunes for defense of the country. Virginia bestirred herself to raise her quota of the 100,000 troops called for by President Jefferson, and the participants in the Burr trial could look from the open windows of the Capitol at the soldiers drilling in the square. Upon refusal of the British war vessels to leave American waters, in accordance with the President's proclamation of July 2d, the American troops were ordered to Hampton Roads to prevent an invasion. Governor Cabell sent the Richmond Cavalry, Captain James Sheppard; the Richmond Light Infantry Blues, Captain William Richardson; and the Republican Blues, Captain Peyton Randolph, to Norfolk—where they remained until the ships sailed away, on July 28th.

The war scare aroused Richmond to the importance of ceasing to depend on English goods and in the following June a meeting to encourage home manufactures was held in the Capitol, with James Monroe as chairman. The Fourth of July was celebrated with fresh enthusiasm that year, with a military parade, and a public dinner at Haymarket Garden, at which Governor Cabell and other citizens clad in homespun to show their independence of foreign goods, made patriotic toasts. Another benefit from the war scare was the bringing together of all political factions into one brotherhood of Americans who forgot for a time their party and personal differences. This was presidential-election year and both candidates—Madison and Monroe—were Virginians, and were familiar figures in the homes, the taverns, the Capitol, and on the streets of Richmond. The great Madison was elected. Monroe's time was not yet come. In January, 1811, he succeeded John Tyler as Governor of Virginia, but for a brief period, for in April, President Madison appointed him Secretary of State and Lieutenant Governor George William Smith became Governor.

CHAPTER XIV

THE THEATRE FIRE

ONE of the pleasures of Richmond in the fall of 1811, was afforded by the Placide Stock Company of players in the new brick theatre, on Academy Square. A star of this company was the young widow, Elizabeth Arnold Poe, whose appearance on the street accompanied by her two pretty children heightened interest in her charming singing, dancing and acting. Her illness and death in her lodgings on Main Street removed her from the boards, and made Richmond, though not the birthplace, the place of earliest recollection and the first home of America's greatest literary genius. She was buried in St. John's Churchyard and her son Edgar, aged two years and ten months, was adopted by John Allan a prominent merchant, and his wife, Frances Valentine, whose beauty has been preserved by the brush of Sully.

The Stock Company continued to appear and on Wednesday night, December 26th, the town was agog over a benefit performance for Mr. Placide. Society turned out in holiday mood and holiday attire and " all went merry as a marriage bell " until the curtain rose for the second act of the after piece. Then, instead of the expected lines, came the terrifying announcement: " The house is on fire! " After an hour of pandemonium marked by deeds of the highest heroism of which human beings are capable —when self is forgotten in a passion for service and even the instinct for self-preservation is lost—the building was a smouldering ash-heap, nearly a hundred of Richmond's 10,000 inhabitants had met a death of agony and many

THE BURNING OF THE RICHMOND THEATRE, DECEMBER 26, 1811
From an old print

MONUMENTAL CHURCH
Erected in 1814, as a memorial, on the site of the burned theatre

others were seriously injured. The newly-elected Governor and U. S. Senator Abram B. Venable were among the victims. Governor Smith was one of those who nobly lost his life in the struggle to save others, while Gilbert Hunt, negro blacksmith—after bearing a great part in the rescue work—escaped. The giant Gilbert and the almost equally powerful Dr. James D. McCaw worked together—Doctor McCaw seizing woman after woman and dropping her from a window to the brawny arms of Gilbert on the ground below. When the walls were about to fall Doctor McCaw dropped from the window himself, but was lamed for life by the fall. When the penitentiary was on fire some years later, Gilbert made a ladder of himself and assisted in rescuing the prisoners. Robert Greenhow, a survivor of the theatre fire left a graphic picture of it in a letter. He and his wife and small son were in a box. Her first words after the alarm was given, and the last he ever heard her speak were: " Save my child!" Almost suffocated with smoke, but with the boy held tight in his arms, he was thrown down and trampled on by the crowd. Let him tell his own story: " When we were kicked to the head of the staircase, finding myself there still prostrate, not being able to rise, I gave my body a sudden impulse that carried us over the dead and dying bodies and pieces of flaming wood that the steps were crowded with, and in that manner, with him in my arms, got to the lower floor, when reanimated by the air rushing in at the doors, I got up and most miraculously, and unhurt, placed myself and child out of danger." He rushed back into the burning building to look for his wife, whom his brother, Doctor Greenhow, had taken under his care, but it was too late.

Another survivor tells of tearing the flaming garments from a woman, wrapping her nude, seared body in his cloak and taking her to a neighboring house and to safety. Lovely Sally Conyers and her fiancé, Lieutenant James Gibbon, U. S. N. (son of Major Gibbon, hero of Stony Point), were in different boxes. Tradition says they had had a misunderstanding and that her escort for the evening was his rival but, at the first alarm Lieutenant Gibbon made his way to her, clasped her in his arms and tried to carry her out of the building. It was not to be, but who will dare say that that wild moment held not for them a wild joy as—reconciled—they perished together, heart on heart and lip on lip.

The whole country mourned. The United States Senate wore crêpe arm-bands for a month. Resolutions of sympathy poured in from all directions and special sermons were preached in distant cities. Stricken Richmond held a mass-meeting in the Capitol on the day after the disaster. It appointed the next Wednesday as a day of fasting and prayer, requested the people to wear crêpe for thirty days, and created a committee with Chief Justice Marshall as chairman to collect funds for a monument. The Common Hall, as the city council was called, closed business places for forty-eight hours, prohibited public shows and balls for four months, and ordered the purchase, by the city, of the theatre site, " to be consecrated as the sacred deposit of the ashes of the victims and enclosed within suitable walls of brick." Later, in joint session, the Monument Committee, a committee from the Common Hall and one from the " Association for the Building of a Church on Shockoe Hill ", decided that the Memorial should take the form of " a Monumental Church . . . to be forever kept sacred for the purpose of Divine worship." The city appropriated $5,000 as its share of the expense and people generally subscribed. The corner-stone was laid on August 4, 1812, under direction of Robert Mills of

By Courtesy of Mrs. Munford

THE HOME OF MRS. BEVERLY BLAND MUNFORD, ORIGINALLY THE WARWICK HOUSE

THE WOMAN'S CLUB, ORIGINALLY THE HAXALL HOUSE

THE HOME OF ELLEN GLASGOW

THE THEATRE FIRE

Washington—the architect chosen—and the church was finished in the spring of 1814. On the monument in its porch were inscribed seventy-two names of those whose ashes were known to lie beneath its floors. It was believed that there were visitors to the city and others who could not be identified. The roll includes persons from every walk of life, but to Death all men are equals and the Fire Fiend is no respecter of persons. In that pyre the ashes of human beings of every rank commingled, and on the marble the names of all—of governor and " stranger ", of senator and carpenter, of brilliant lawyer and bootmaker, of author of the play and actress, of beauty dying in the arms of the lover striving frantically to save her, of slave woman and of free negress are written indiscriminately. There is no suggestion of precedence or of classification.

In November, 1813, Bushrod Washington, then living at Mt. Vernon, and Edmund J. Lee, of Alexandria, approached Rev. Richard Channing Moore, D. D., of New York, in regard to taking charge of the Episcopal church then building at Richmond, with intention of making him Bishop of Virginia. In May, 1814, he was called by the Monumental Church and the Diocese, and was consecrated Bishop in Philadelphia. In him the circle of Judge Marshall acquired a new kindred spirit and Richmond a citizen whose influence in the development of what is highest and best in her life was immeasurable. Among pews marked with names of their earliest owners are that in which Judge Marshall sat with his large family—unlatching its door during prayers to enable his long legs to protrude into the aisle, and that of John Allan from which Edgar Poe—a wistful-eyed lad with chestnut ringlets—spelled out the words, " Give Ear O Lord ", in big, golden letters above the chancel. Lafayette, from a seat in the Marshall pew, on the Sunday he spent in Richmond in

1824, was one of a long procession of worshippers of every class and condition that have since read this legend, which still contributes to the atmosphere of solemnity with which all who visit Monumental Church are impressed. To appreciate the sacrifices which were brought into the fabric of this interesting memorial it must be remembered that it was erected during the hard times which always accompany war. Its construction was almost exactly coincident with the war of 1812—having been projected a short time before that war was declared and finished a short time before peace was proclaimed.

CHAPTER XV

THE WAR OF 1812

In the summer of 1809 Mr. Thomas Rutherfoord, returning home to Richmond with his wife and daughter in their family carriage from the White Sulphur and Sweet Springs, spent a day at Monticello. Monroe was visiting there, and Mr. Rutherfoord heard Jefferson say to him: "We shall never be on good terms with England until we have had a brush with her." When, on June 18, 1812, war was, at last, declared, and President Madison asked for volunteers, Governor Barbour called for Richmond's quota and Richmond responded. On the Fourth of July the Governor, in uniform, read the Declaration of Independence and President Madison's message to a great gathering of the people, including the military companies, in Capitol Square, and that night every house in the intensely patriotic city was illuminated. The Twentieth Regiment, with two Richmond companies, was ordered to Albany to protect the northern and western frontiers and the Square became a busy scene with people preparing tents, knapsacks and so on, for the soldiers, in addition to the drilling. Outside of town the powder mills worked overtime. In December, news that the English fleet was threatening Norfolk and might come on to Richmond created great excitement. The Governor ordered the Nineteenth Regiment to Norfolk, many of whose citizens took refuge in Richmond. A committee was appointed to find them homes and a home guard consisting largely of Revolutionary veterans was formed. Richmond was the rendezvous for troops from the great western section of Virginia marching toward Norfolk and the sea-coast, and the fields beyond town were covered with tents.

In the midst of war time Richmond was gay. A year had gone by since the theatre fire and Mr. Rutherfoord noted in his diary that there never was a winter of greater festivities than that of 1812-13. And the city was going forward. A public library and a marine insurance company were included in the new enterprises and the *Compiler*—Richmond's earliest daily paper—was born, to die in infancy. The Virginia Bible Society, founded in July, 1813, showed a more robust constitution, and is still active. Two new stage lines were started. Coaches over one of them left Richmond daily, each one arriving in Washington on the third day later. Others left Washington daily, arriving in Richmond on the third day later —six days for the round trip. The line between Richmond and Lynchburg required a week for the round trip. The stages kept innumerable taverns going and many stories have been told of this informal kind of travel and of wayside hospitality. On the Lynchburg route, not far from Richmond, was " Midlothian "—the private residence of Abraham S. Wooldridge, a major of the War of 1812. His hospitality was so proverbial that occasionally a stage driver would suggest to his passengers to stop by " Midlothian " for a julep. A hearty welcome from the Major always added flavor to the fragrant refreshment.

In June, 1813, came the news that the British had attacked Craney Island at the mouth of Norfolk harbor and would come on to Richmond. The alarm rang out from the Bell Tower, and was boomed by cannon. Every citizen who could bear arms was called into service and " old men of sixty were seen stepping into the ranks." The Blues and Rifles overflowed with recruits and in four

110

hours a company of Flying Artillery was organized, with William Wirt as Captain. A faded old letter says: " The ladies were busy sending good food to camp for the soldiers and inviting all who could be spared to dine." (How history repeats itself!) Fort Powhatan and Fort Malvern Hill were garrisoned and Camp Holly Springs—Gen. J. H. Cocke, Commander—was established to defend Virginia's Capitol, if need be. The cloud passed over, but war times made hard times. The blockade made it impossible to ship tobacco, flour and other produce abroad, and they became a drug on the market. Dr. Thomas Massie, an army surgeon, with a bad case of blues, writing from Richmond to his father in Nelson County, says: " The best mode of disposing of any kind of grain at present is to distil it into whiskey, that liquor, I am informed being worth 90 cents per gallon. Wheat and flour are almost worth nothing at present. . . . Military service, rotting crops and heavy taxes will put their (the people's) democracy to the test."

Depression in Richmond was increased by repeated successes of the British in the northwest, but publication in the *Enquirer* of September 21, 1813, of the epigrammatic message, " We have met the enemy and they are ours ", in which Commodore Perry announced his victory at Lake Erie brought great rejoicing. Mayor Greenhow appointed a day of thanksgiving, when sermons were preached by Parson Blair at the Capitol and Parson Jacob Gregg at the Baptist " Meeting House."

In March, 1814, the *Enquirer* announced the threat of Massachusetts to " secede and thus destroy the Union " because the war with England was not brought to an end. " How unlike Virginia ", exclaimed the shocked editor, " who flew to the aid of Massachusetts when, in '76, the British made their attack on Boston! "

RICHMOND: ITS PEOPLE AND ITS STORY

In the summer of this year when the British entered Washington and burned the Capitol and the White House, and also did much damage in the neighborhood of the birthplaces of Washington and Lee, in the Northern Neck of Virginia, it was again rumored that they were on their way to Richmond. The Blues (under Captain Murphy, whom we have seen making holiday with the Two Parsons), Captain Stevenson's Artillery, and Captain Taylor's Rifles, were called into service, and Virginia's sons flocked from every direction to defend their beloved Capital. In companies and singly they came—"the mountaineer with his rifle, the fisherman with his gun and the citizen with his arms." On horseback and on foot they journeyed through the blistering heat—some barefooted, with their shoes hanging over their guns. Many heads of families took their wives and children out of town— some of them to the Springs. On July 16th, Doctor Massie wrote: "I do not think it improbable that Richmond will be a pile of ashes before the fall." On September 5th, he recorded: "The town is in consternation, most of the inhabitants gone." And on September 13th: "Money scarce. The country is almost in a state of destitution." Again the cloud passed over, but the militia and volunteer companies kept Richmond surrounded until December, when reports of peace negotiations at Ghent brought relief from the anxiety. News of Gen. Andrew Jackson's great victory at New Orleans (on January 8th), followed by the ratification of the Treaty of Ghent (on February 17th), and President Madison's proclamation of peace (on February 18, 1815), brought a succession of joys. At the order of Mayor Thomas Wilson, the Capitol and all the houses in town were illuminated on the night of March 1st, and there was a mile-long procession of soldiers and citizens carrying transparencies. There was another demonstration, but of a social character, to welcome Gen. Winfield Scott to the city in December 1817. During his visit the young general captured the heart of one of Richmond's belles—Maria Mayo, daughter of Col. John Mayo of " The Hermitage ", where their marriage in the early spring was a fashionable event. General Scott failed to hold Richmond's affection to the end of of his life—but that is another story.

Among the first signs of progress to follow in the wake of peace was a steamboat on James River to ply between Richmond and Norfolk. She made a trial trip to Warwick, with a party of ladies and gentlemen aboard, on June 22, 1815. " With wind and tide, she moved at the rate of four miles an hour ", according to the newspaper account, but on the return trip against the tide—made only two miles. " She turns, she runs backward as well as forward with wonderful ease. All those who saw the splendid stranger hailed her with enthusiasm ", announces the delighted paper.

A forward movement of the following year was the beginning of the present public school system, when a " Lancasterian school ", named for the father of public schools in England, was established opposite the jail. In it " children of the wealthy were taught at the most reasonable rates and the children of the poor gratis." The city gave the lot with $5000 for a building, and an endowment of $600 a year, and the people added liberal subscriptions.

PART V
PEACEFUL AND PROSPEROUS YEARS
(1820-1859)

CHAPTER XVI

LAFAYETTE!

Now in Richmond, with a population of something over 12,000 people, nearly half of whom are negroes, follows scene after scene telling a story of activity and development in business, civic and social life. There are set-backs, but the general tendency is toward growth. New mercantile enterprises are started to succeed or to fail, new discoveries and inventions are tried out, new churches and schools built. Meetings in behalf of public education and of organizations philanthropic, cultural and recreational are held. As time goes on, many whose faces have so long been familiar that they seem as much a part of the place as its houses and trees are missed, and the mournful pageant of hearse and hack announces that they have passed out forever. New actors fill their places and it would seem that every trace of those who have made their exit would soon be lost. But Memory persists in living on and entrusts to Tradition curiously indestructible stuff. Newspapers, fluttering in the grasp of eager readers one day to disappear the next, like yesterday's butterflies, come out of their hiding places in the course of time—limp, *café-au-lait* colored, and perhaps dilapidated, but still decipherable, and persons and events buried in their columns come forth and live again. The attic of an old house about to be demolished gives up a small sole-leather trunk which holds a bundle of letters designed by those who penned them for prompt destruction. Their long since broken seals are crumbling, the faded and rotting ribbon which binds them breaks at a touch, they are carefully unfolded and smoothed out and their dim writing exposes all they have to tell to the eyes of a new generation. A panel between the pigeon-holes of an ancient desk is accidentally moved, revealing a secret drawer. Within lies a diary kept for the private perusal of its writer. Like the newspapers and the letters, it throws a flood of light on long forgotten scenes from real life, and raises from the dead the men and women who enacted them.

Such sources, and others, show that more or less exciting incidents broke the normal routine of life in Richmond from time to time. In the summer of 1820, the city opened its hearts and homes to refugees from the Norfolk yellow fever scourge. Three years and a half later its ready compassion was touched by an appeal from much further away. Lord Byron was the poet of the hour. Stirred by his trumpet call:

> "The isles of Greece, the isles of Greece,
> Where burning Sappho loved and sung."

and by other poems written to arouse interest in the struggle of the Greeks to free themselves from Turkish despotism, Richmond people gathered in the Capitol (where the General Assembly was in session), and with Linn Banks, Speaker of the House, as president of the meeting, and Thomas Ritchie, founder of the *Enquirer*, as secretary, passed resolutions of sympathy for the oppressed people and named a committee to raise money for their cause.

The year was 1824, the month was October and the day (which had been eagerly awaited) was the 26th—a cold, grizzly, drizzly day, but the wooded river-banks and the embowering foliage within town glowed with autumnal color and smiling faces of home folk and visitors who packed every nook and corner testified that Richmond was filled with a kind of sunshine which did not depend

118

LINDEN ROW, FRANKLIN STREET

Occupying a block of what was for several generations the heart of fashionable Richmond. The fourth house from the right was
"The Long Roll" and others of her best known books. From a photograph by Mr. Searing T

BROAD STREET BETWEEN SEVENTH AND EIGHTH IN 1865

...sting Marshall Theatre and the Richmond, Fredericksburg and Potomac train going down the middle of the street

From an old print

on weather. Along Ninth Street from Main to Broad
was a series of evergreen arches. In Capitol Square were
other arches bearing the names of Washington, Lafayette,
Nelson, Green, Morgan, Wayne and Mercer. One of
them was at the Grace Street gate, one at the Tenth
Street gate, another at the gate leading to the Governor's
Mansion; the rest were in the middle of the Square. On
either side of Lafayette's arch stood an obelisk inscribed
with the names of his compatriots of the Revolution.
Down on Main and Twelfth Streets the courtyard of
Eagle Hotel had been floored over and canopied with canvas, providing a huge ball room. Approach to it was
under an arch, erected by "the Ladies." A suite of
rooms for the city's guest of honor had been engaged in
the hotel, and twenty additional rooms for other officers
of the Revolution. Further down town " the military and
an immense multitude " thronged the wharves and the
heights overlooking them.

The Norfolk steamer at last! On deck a white-haired
man of soldierly bearing, clad in cocked hat and shorts
was the centre of a group of Richmond's best who had
met and boarded the steamer a few miles down the river,
and with whom he chatted with animation of expression
and gesture characteristic of the French. As he stepped
upon the landing and was escorted to a carriage drawn
by four prancing white horses, the artillery saluted and
the people cheered. In the carriage with him were Hon.
John C. Calhoun and two of the welcoming committee.
The Fayette Guard marched in front of the carriage and
then came young George Washington Layafette- his carriage drawn by " four splendid greys." Other carriages
filled with dignitaries, officers of the Revolution, and so
on, came next. The artillery followed and a " pretty-
looking company of small boys dressed in hunting shirts

and styling themselves the 'Morgan Legion'", brought up the rear.

The procession, followed by "a numerous mass" of people on horse or afoot halted at Union Hotel, under a double arch garlanded with evergreens, at each of whose four bases stood a living statue—a beautiful young girl. Then, on to the "Eagle"! Here General Lafayette was greeted by forty officers of the American Revolution— his comrades in arms of forty-odd years before.

At five o'clock the guests and their hosts sat down to a great public banquet—Benjamin Watkins Leigh presiding. It was a feast of sentiment as well as good food and drink. Reminiscence held full sway—now growing tender, now merry, as the company was led back through more than two score years. Rattling good stories made them hold their sides, thrilling bits of romance and flavorsome morsels of gossip were drawn from Memory's storehouse. Toasts were drunk in mellow old wine. "Health to our great friend and beloved guest," was given with a shout. "The memory of Washington" in muffled tone— while all stood. Lafayette himself gave "The State of Virginia: The City of Richmond", in his quaint, slightly broken English. Not until eleven o'clock did the diners rise after six hours at what was to go down in history as the most memorable and longest dinner ever given in Richmond.

Next day there was a great parade of military, members of the Cincinnati, and citizens, including all of the local ministers. Two faces were missed—Parsons Blair and Buchanan had died within a few weeks of each other somewhat less than three years before. Sidewalks, porches and windows along the line of march were filled with happy faces. "Handkerchiefs and hats waved on all sides like the leaves of a forest in a gale of wind and the eager shouts of welcome filling the air rose high above martial music." At the City Hall, Mayor John Adams, on one side of whose seat hung a portrait of Washington on the other side one of Lafayette (which may be seen to-day in the present City Hall, on the same site) made an address of welcome. He saluted the hero of the hour as " a fellow citizen of Virginia and a brother by adoption." Lafayette's response was brief but eloquent. He was next taken across the street into the Capitol Square where many of his old comrades awaited him. Chief Justice Marshall was their spokesman. Lafayette replied:

" My dear companions-in-arms, I had anticipated the pleasure to meet many of you in the Metropolis of Virginia, and I enjoy it with delight." He reminded them that " the four gallant Virginia Lines—Virginia Continentals, riflemen, volunteer corps and militia " were his first command in the Army. Some of these old men, as well as many of the women and children who crowded about him were greeted with the picturesque French kiss first on one cheek then the other. The large number of ladies whom having been " kissed by Lafayette in '24, my dear!" surrounded with an aura of romance distinctly perceptible to themselves and almost visible to others, long contributed a sentimental tinge to Richmond's atmosphere.

Lafayette and the other Revolutionary veterans were the dinner guests of Governor Pleasants, at the Mansion, and refreshments were brought out and distributed among the multitude in the Square. After dinner the General reviewed the troops from the porch of Mr. James Lyons and at night drove through a town brilliant with illu minations and fireworks, to the theatre. The audience greeted him with thunders of applause and the orchestra played " Auld Lang Syne " with " thrilling effect."

During the next morning he received about five hundred Sunday School children in the " Eagle's " big tent, smiling benignly into eyes soft with worshipful wonder and brushing pure cheeks with his lips, and afterward visited Harmony Hall School. Later in the day he drove in the carriage with its four white horses to the Tree Hill races, and dined with the Jockey Club.

Dear to the heart of the early Virginian was horse-flesh—especially thoroughbred, racing horseflesh. Gentlemen of highest social standing and greatest wealth were proud owners of noted racers, and their rivalry as to the appearance and behavior of their fleet-footed darlings added to the excitement and fascination of this most popular sport of the period. Racing was, indeed, the old time Virginian's base-ball, foot-ball and golf combined. It has been written that the death of the famous thoroughbred, " Diomed ", in 1808, caused almost as much mourning as that of General Washington in 1799. During the first two or three decades of the nineteenth century Richmond was the greatest racing centre of the United States. To its three tracks—Tree Hill, Fairfield and Broadrock—came, in spring and fall the most famous horses from all parts of the country. Here ran " Sir Archy ", " Florizel ", " Wrangler ", " Lady Lightfoot ", " Virginian ", " Sir Charles ", " Flirtilla ", " Sir Henry ", " Bonnets o' Blue ", " Boston " and many others of almost equal note. For years the most widely known and successful American turfman of his time was William R. Johnson, of Chesterfield County (across the river from Richmond) and his best horses were constantly seen on the Richmond tracks.

The principal race—four mile heats—of the day on which Lafayette was at Tree Hill, was won by " Virginia ", one of Mr. Johnson's racers. According to a story handed down by an eye witness, the winner was, after the race, led up and put through her paces for the benefit of the distinguished guest, who was told by her owner that henceforth her name would be " Virginia Lafayette."

That night the General was guest of honor at the ball in the Eagle's improvised ballroom, which floral and evergreen decorations, banners and twinkling lights had turned into a fairyland, and whose floor of 8000 square feet was crowded. On Friday, October 29th, Petersburg gave him a joyful reception. On Saturday he was back in Richmond, at a dinner given by the Masons of Richmond and Manchester—" Right Worshipful John Marshall " presiding. On Sunday, sitting in the Marshall pew at Monumental church, he heard Bishop Moore preach, and doubtless held a reception on the roomy church porch afterward.

A few years later Richmond heard with delight that France had become a republic and that the Marquis de la Fayette was once more at the head of the French National Guards, and on September 11, 1831, gave vent to its satisfaction with (of course) a military parade and salute, an address at the Capitol (by Wyndham Robertson) and an illumination at night.

None enjoyed the festivities in Lafayette's honor more than the ebon-skinned coachmen whose part it was to convey their " white folks " thither. The delightful physiognomy and genial smile of one of these at a later period in his life, has been preserved. On that memorable 28th of October 1824 " Uncle Henry "—then in his prime— drove his " ole Marster " and " Mistiss "—the Mann S. Valentines—to the races and ball, in the family carriage. In his old age his " young Marster " modelled a bust of him now to be seen in the Valentine Museum.

It has been said of America's child-race, the negroes, that they will follow men marching to a band anywhere,

123

at any time. The love of Richmond, white and black, for processions was doubtless evidence of its freshness of spirit—its unsophistication. On an August Friday of 1827, its people lined Main Street to witness the most gruesome bit of pageantry in the city's history. Three mysterious figures, hooded and gowned in purple and with ropes around their necks were led from the county jail on lower Main Street to a wagon holding three coffins. They were Spanish pirates under sentence of death. Each seated upon the grim box in which his body was soon to lie, the purple-shrouded figures were driven, under military guard, through town to the penitentiary where the gallows waited, and where the encircling hills provided a gallery for a great throng of spectators.

CHAPTER XVII

A NEW CONSTITUTION

THE Constitutional Convention was the absorbing event of the year 1829, and drew many visitors not only from the neighborhood and beyond, but from distant states, "on to Richmond." Newspapers had made the names of the delegates known to the whole country. Among them were two men who had been United States Presidents (Madison and Monroe); the great Chief Justice; one who was to be a president, and others who had been, were, or were on the road to be members of the United States Senate and House of Representatives; governors of Virginia; judges of the United States Supreme Court and of the Virginia Court of Appeals, and lawyers of national reputation.

The spread of Virginia's population to the westward and the growing feeling of democracy had, almost from the time of the Revolution, caused demand for a convention to bring the State Constitution into accord with new ideas. Its opening session was in the Hall of the House of Delegates, on October 8th, but most of its later ones were held in the old First African Church, at the corner below Monumental. There it sat while the soft winds of Indian summer stripped the trees leaf by leaf of their gay autumn vesture until they were black and bare, and through days of winter sunshine and winter rain and winter snow until January 14, 1830, when the new Constitution—ratified by the people at the spring elections— was adopted. There was present one man, and one only, who had helped to frame both Virginia's first Constitution, in 1776, and later, the Constitution of the United States

—the snowy haired James Madison. He was now the first speaker—rising to nominate James Monroe to be President of the Convention. Monroe was unanimously elected and Madison and Marshall ceremoniously escorted him to the chair. Later, impaired health made it necessary for him to resign and Philip P. Barbour succeeded him. The graphic letter of an eye witness aids newspaper reports in letting us see, at this late day, the new Constitution in the making. Madison was " a small man of ample forehead and some obliquity of vision . . . His dress was plain his overcoat a faded brown surtout." It is a healthy thing for a period which seems to think that only youth must be served, and to have forgotten how little true worth depends on externals, to read that " When he rose a great part of the members left their seats and clustered around the aged statesman like a swarm of bees." His voice was extremely low but when he spoke " a pin might have been heard to drop." Monroe—always a homely man—was " very wrinkled and weather-beaten, ungraceful in attitude and gesture ", but none the less revered. Judge Marshall, " tall, in a long surtout of blue and with an eye of fire ", appeared " revolutionary and patriarchal." He " possessed the rare faculty of condensation; he distilled an argument down to its essence." Governor Giles " wore a crutch." His style of oratory was " conversational—no gestures—no effort, but . . . his words were like honey pouring from an eastern rock."

The Convention was divided into two parties—the eastern or conservative, led by Benjamin Watkins Leigh, and the western, or radical, by Chapman Johnson—two of the most brilliant lawyers and orators of their time. Leigh was slight, graceful and handsome, Johnson of noble and commanding presence and strikingly benevolent countenance. The Constitution was taken up section

AVENUE OF LINDENS ON THE BOULEVARD, APPROACHING WILLIAM BYRD PARK

LAKE IN JOSEPH BRYAN PARK

A RICHMOND "MAMMY" FOR THREE GENERATIONS, WITH ONE OF HER
"CHILDREN" AS A BRIDE OF 1922

By permission

A NEW CONSTITUTION

by section and the debates on the amendments were for the most part contests between the two parties—between East and West—between conservatism and advancing democracy.

Hugh Rose Pleasants—a newspaper writer and man of letters of the day, and brother of John Hampden Pleasants—writing in the *Southern Literary Messenger*, calls John Randolph of " Roanoke " the " hero " of the Convention. " He was known to be an unrivalled orator ", but as yet, he had been heard by comparatively few Virginians. His career had been national and he had never been in the State Legislature. " The anxiety to hear him among all classes of persons, strangers as well as citizens, amounted almost to phrenzy. . . It was expected that he would answer Chapman Johnson's first great speech and a crowd thronged the Capitol such as we never saw there before, and never expect to see again. Ladies were absolutely packed into the galleries and the spare seats in the Hall. There was no room even to breathe." But Randolph did not speak. At last, on a day when " nobody expected it—when the lobby and the galleries were almost deserted —Randolph rose slowly from his seat and pronounced the words, 'Mr. President!' . . . Where the crowd came from or how they got intelligence that Randolph had the floor we could never learn. But it poured in like the waters of the ocean when the dyke gives way. Persons who were on the streets, afterwards informed us that they saw persons running from all quarters, and not being able to find where they were running to, fell in with, and assisted to form the multitude that streamed to the Capitol . . . . The unaccountable brilliancy of Mr. Randolph's eyes—their petrifying effect upon those on whom he chose to fix them, in anger or disdain, the melody of his inimitable voice—his tall unearthly looking figure, and the

127

shape of his bony finger have been described; but no man who never heard him and saw him speak can form the slightest conception of what he was."

Among the group gathered about the reporters' table listening intently and scribbling busily, were two Richmond men widely known throughout Virginia and far beyond its borders—men of independent mind and interesting personality. They were John Hampden Pleasants, editor of *The Whig,* and Thomas Ritchie, Sr., founder of the democratic paper, *The Enquirer.* Both were prominent socially and powerful politically, both were stubbornly partizan— and of course they were natural enemies. As they sat at the same table making notes for their respective papers interest in them would have increased a thousand fold if any seer of the future could have arisen to foretell a day when one of them would die by the hand of a son of the other.

On the night of St. Valentine's eve, 1830, a month less a day after adjournment of the Convention, an echo of the noise it made in its world was heard in the name of the packet boat *Constitution,* which arrived from Lynchburg with twenty shivering but happy passengers. Richmond welcomed, warmed and fed them, and joyfully celebrated the successful beginning of canal transportation between the two cities. Two years later the Legislature granted to the James River and Kanawha Company a charter to connect the river James with the Ohio. A committee, with Chief Justice Marshall as chairman, was appointed to dispose of stock, and the Bank of Virginia, the Common Hall and citizens of Richmond, together subscribed to more than a million dollars worth.

The canal tow-path was destined to become redolent of love's young dreams and doubtless of lover's quarrels, too. Lying between the river—dashing boisterously over rocks and swirling around green, willow-fringed islets (on the left) and (on the right) the untroubled waters of the canal, silently flowing beneath a bluff overhung by trees and festooned with a tangle of vines through which gleamed, in season, a profusion of wild violets, heartsease and blue-eyed periwinkles, it provided a picturesque and romantic walk. This was for many years as favorite a resort of Richmond's belles and beaux as the fashionable elm-shaded promenade along the elevated and grassy river-bank, for some distance down stream from Fifteenth Street—now in the heart of the busy wholesale and manu-facturing section—had been at the beginning of the century.

CHAPTER XVIII

THE NEGRO PROBLEM

RICHMOND had now grown to over 16,000 inhabitants, but more than half of them were negroes—a fact which contributed largely to the alarm created by the "Nat Turner Insurrection", in Southampton County. Turner was a negro preacher under whose leadership sixty-four white people, for the most part women and children, were murdered by members of his race who had been to a camp meeting on a Sunday night in August, 1831. The whole State was thrown into a panic, for no one knew how general the plot might be. Richmond sent troops to Southampton and organized a home guard to patrol the streets at night during the absence of the military.

On December 29, 1831—only four months after the insurrection—the Virginia Historical Society was formed in the Capitol (with a constitution drawn by George Tucker, and with John Marshall as president and Governor Floyd vice-president) and the meeting may serve as a sign post that normal conditions had been established for the time being.

But the Negro question had long been causing anxiety in Richmond and the end was not yet. The difficult question of abolition was being agitated and anti-slavery societies were sending their literature to the negroes. In 1835, Richmond's uneasiness was increased by reports of a serious insurrection in Mississippi. "Incendiaries", as northern abolitionists who urged the slaves to desperate deeds were called, were busy, but in Boston, New York and other northern cities meetings condemning their practices were held. Richmonders made a bonfire of some of their pamphlets, on Main Street in front of the post-office. As early as 1824, a Colonization Society had been organized (with Chief Justice Marshall, president, and Governor James Pleasants, vice-president) as an auxiliary to the American Society to provide homes on the eastern coast of Africa for free negroes who, strange as it may seem, were held in contempt by slaves, basking in reflected importance varying in degree according to the social prominence of their owners. At the time of the Nat Turner Insurrection nearly 2000 of Richmond's dark skinned population were free negroes. Many of these were finally settled in the land of their forefathers. In one year—1853—the Virginia Colonization Society sent 243 of them to Liberia and raised $10,925—the largest amount subscribed for the purpose in any state.

In September of the year 1833, a cholera epidemic brought woe and death and paralyzed business. Those who could flee to safety did so, but all the physicians and clergymen remained at their posts in the suffering city, ministering to stricken humanity—a great majority of whom were of the dark race.

In every home in Richmond two men, the family pastor and the family physician received into sympathetic ears all the joys and sorrows of the house and were on intimate terms with the skeletons in its closets.

In them Democracy found its fullest expression. Since bodies stripped of finery were simply bodies, and souls with pretense laid by were simply souls, people were simply people, and the doctors and the parsons ministered to all alike—white and black. The sunshine they carried about with them was infectious. At the sight of their faces, the sound of their voices and their warm hand-pressure the sufferer took heart. If his pain was not at once lessened it became, at least, easier to bear, and when at the end of the visit the little stories of which both doctor and minister had an inexhaustible supply, were brought out, the hearer, like " Tommy Grace " with the " pain in his face ", was sure to laugh and find himself growing better.

CHAPTER XIX

HAPS AND MISHAPS

In the year 1832 Richmond ceased to depend on wells and springs for its drinking water and saw the completion of a pumphouse and reservoir. True, the then unfiltered James River product looked more like wine than water, but having it piped into homes soon made possible in Richmond that interesting novelty and aid to comfort and civilization—the bath-tub.

In November 1833, consternation caused by the great shower of stars which negroes picturesquely termed "snowing fire" was followed by the less spectacular financial panic which lasted through the following year. It was one of those periods when money—or the lack of it—was more discussed in homes and taverns than ailments or the weather. Relief came at length and a new but cheerful epidemic made its appearance—one of railroad building. Soon amazing iron horses came clanging their bells and shrieking and snorting demoniacally into town, with strings of stuffy little coaches clattering after them.

Scene: A dark stairway in any house in Richmond, up which children light themselves to bed with sputtering candles in brass candle sticks, and singing:

> "Little Nan Etticoat, in a white petticoat,
> The longer she stands, the shorter she grows."

Scene: Any thoroughfare in Richmond after nightfall. Enter citizens shouting: "Let us have light, now we grope in darkness through our rugged and dangerous streets. Let us have light!"

Not until 1846 did the City Council listen to the people's complaint. Plans were then set afoot for City Gas Works and the passing bell of " Nan Etticoat " began to toll.

In the following year the first telegram ever received in Richmond came from Washington, and the city marvelled almost as solemnly and as long as it would today if it should have a message from Mars.

In 1838 Richmond indulged in a get-rich-quick dream. Everybody's spare cash (and much that could not be spared) was turned into mulberry trees and silk-worm eggs, with the certainty that a crop of silk-worms equal to a gold mine would be the result. Their gain was in wisdom instead of coin. The vaccination was not lasting enough, however, to give immunity from the real gold fever when Richmond (which had then a population of 30,000) sent many " forty-niners ", as they were called, westward, ho! to California—some of them equipped with pick, shovel and frying pan that they might lose no time in experiencing the thrilling sensation of digging and washing the sparkling ore.

In the summer of 1850 the first of many, many. made-in-Richmond locomotives shipped to various places, in both America and Europe, was built for the Richmond and Danville Railroad Company.

But we go too fast. Let us turn back for a nearer view of some of the scenes that stand out clear against the background which has been hastily sketched.

CHAPTER XX

POE AND " THE MESSENGER "

In 1834 appeared *The Southern Literary Messenger* —a magazine " devoted to every department of literature and the fine arts, published in Richmond by T. W. White, every fortnight, $5 per annum."

Early in the year 1835, John P. Kennedy, of Baltimore, wrote to Mr. White calling his attention to " a remarkable young man by the name of Edgar Poe."

Jefferson's dream of the University of Virginia had come true years before this time and Poe had been one of the Richmond boys to whom it promptly became Alma Mater. The seventeen-year-old genius suddenly freed from every restraint, at the weakest period of a boy's life, distinguished himself there as a student—but sowed some wild oats. The small amount of money with which his foster father believed it prudent to supply him caused gambling to be the most irresistible of the temptations which assailed him. Everybody knows the result. At the end of one term Poe was back in Richmond once more, at the Randolph mansion, on Main Street at Fifth (which the Allans had lately purchased), with all hope of completing his education forfeited. For a short time his romantic face was seen about Richmond, but though he had a few devoted admirers, nobody recognized him as the world-poet-to-be and to many he was only that wild, bad boy whom Mr. Allan, in an hour of injudicious benevolence made the mistake of adopting. Soon he became a wanderer. His little world lost sight of him and most Richmond people had forgotten him and his cranks and his pranks when stories and poems and critiques sounding an entirely new note began to appear in the *Messenger*. That magazine's circulation at once increased by leaps and bounds. Followed an invitation from Mr. White to Mr. Poe to become assistant editor. Older, dreamier—at times, " wilder "—slender, black-coated and wearing a tall top hat, he became a familiar figure about Richmond again, with a frail looking, gazelle-eyed, fourteen-year-old girl—his wife—hanging on his arm after the approved, clinging-vine fashion of the day.

Years passed. Edgar Poe had no longer a part in the Richmond scene, but from Philadelphia—from New York—came echoes of his growing fame, and his work in newspapers, in magazines, in small bound volumes, was read in the city of his boyhood, as everywhere else. Some said: " Well, well! So Edgar Poe wrote that! Sounds like real poetry, but I can't forget how drunk he got that night at ' The Swan'. " " No," said another, " nor how he gambled at the University. Such base ingratitude to Mr. Allan! " Others, wagging their heads, took up the censures—made a chorus of them. Old friends raised defending voices: " Edgar wasn't the only college boy that ever gambled, nor the only Richmond boy that ever drank. Remember, it was at Mr. Allan's own table that he learned to drink! He's going to pay back all he owes him in time—he's going to make the Allan name immortal." But The Crowd paid no attention.

Again years passed. In 1849, toward the close of summer, Edgar Poe, the acknowledged literary artist, made holiday in Richmond. The élite of town crowded the assembly rooms of the Exchange Hotel to hear his lectures on " The Philosophy of Composition " and " The Poetic Principle ", and his recitations of " The Raven ", and sat spell-bound while he—erect and still and pale as

EDGAR ALLAN POE, FROM A CRAYON PORTRAIT DRAWN BY
F. J. FISHER ABOUT 1858, FROM A DAGUERREOTYPE OWNED BY
JOHN R. THOMPSON, EDITOR OF THE *SOUTHERN LITERARY
MESSENGER*

Fisher took the portrait to Berlin, where he and Edward V. Valentine and his
brother William Valentine studied art and lived in the same house, and where
the Valentine brothers nursed him through an attack of smallpox. In appreciation, Fisher gave his Poe portrait to Edward V. Valentine who still owns it.
It has never been reproduced until now, when Mr. Valentine has permitted it
to be photographed especially for Mrs. Stanard

EDGAR ALLAN POE SHRINE, REAR VIEW OF THE OLD STONE HOUSE
The oldest building in Richmond, now a museum of Poeana

EDGAR ALLAN POE SHRINE. THE LOGGIA AND GARDEN FROM THE OLD STONE HOUSE
The Loggia was built of material saved from the *Southern Literary Messenger* building

a statue—filled their ears with music and their souls with wonder at the strangeness and the brilliancy of his thought and words.

After Poe's time the *Southern Literary Messenger* continued its honorable career until the end of 1865. John R. Thompson, a less brilliant though worthy man of letters, was long its editor and—as a later editor, and one of its many notable contributors—the genial Dr. George W. Bagby, helped.Richmond to laugh during years when she needed to laugh whenever she could. *The Messenger* building, on Main Street at Fifteenth, was an object of interest until a few years ago when it was condemned and torn down. Its seasoned timbers have been used to restore the woodwork of the " Old Stone House " which in 1922 became the " Edgar Allan Poe Shrine ", and to make cases to hold the Poeana there, and the loggia in the " Shrine " garden was built of some of its bricks and stone. The desk at which Poe laid the foundations of his own fame as well as that of the *Messenger* occupies a place of honor within the " Shrine."

Reference to Poe's child-wife naturally suggests the author of " David Copperfield." On the evening of March 17, 1842, the Washington train brought to Richmond " Mr. Charles Dickens and lady." His books had given Richmond a jolly good time and Richmond paid in kind its debt to the young author in snuff-colored suit and red cravat, and his rather drab and shy " lady ", during their three days' visit. Among quaint toasts at the supper for a hundred guests at the Exchange Hotel, was " Charles Dickens, the ' artful dodger '; he has dodged Philadelphia and Baltimore, but he could not dodge the Old Dominion."

In the early spring of 1853—ten years after Poe's last appearance in Richmond and three and a half after

Dickens' visit—Thackeray was the fêted guest of the city. For at least part of the time his hostess was Mrs. Robert C. Stanard (whose husband had been Poe's schoolmate and chum) in the house which is now the Westmoreland Club. He stayed a week this time, during which he delivered to audiences which packed the Athenæum on Marshall Street, near Eleventh, three lectures on literary subjects: "Swift"; "Congreve and Addison", and "Steele and the Times of Queen Anne." On March 3d, he wrote from Richmond to Mrs. Baxter, of New York, of being "Delighted with the comfortable, friendly, cheery little town—the picturesquest" he had "seen in America." Adding: "I am having a good time—pleasant people, good audiences, quiet, handsome, cheap, comfortable hotel"—evidently the "Exchange."

Richmond was fascinated with the man and his lectures. John R. Thompson, then editor of the *Southern Literary Messenger,* said in that magazine that Thackeray's visit should be marked with a white stone in the city's history. He was invited to repeat his visit on his return from the South, and on March 12th, he wrote from Charleston: "From this I shall go to Richmond most probably, and say my say out there; if their enthusiasm lasts four weeks I am sure of a great welcome at that pretty little cheery place—such a welcome as is better than dollars."

He stayed another week and lectured on "Prior, Gay, and Pope"; "Hogarth, Smollet, and Fielding", and "Sterne and Goldsmith." In January 1856, he spent still another week in Richmond, and gave three lectures on "The Georges of England; Court and Town Life during their Reigns." In February of that year he wrote to Mrs. Baxter from Savannah:

POE AND "THE MESSENGER"

"At Richmond I had a pleasant little time, a very pleasant little time."

During this last stay in Richmond, Thackeray dropped in to see Thompson at his office in the *Messenger* building. While chatting together in that charmed language which men and women steeped in familiarity with books know, Thackeray drew a sheet of paper toward him and scribbled —probably on the desk which had been Poe's and was then Thompson's—the now famous verses—" The Sorrows of Werther "—in which he comically and tersely summed up Goethe's most sentimental story—which was then being widely read. These satirical lines showing the author of "Vanity Fair " in merry mood appeared in the *Messenger* for November 1853, with an editorial note saying, " They have afforded amusement to many friends who have read them in manuscript."

Thackeray died at his home on Christmas Eve 1863, when Richmond, as Capital of the Confederacy, was in the dreadful grip of war. Indications of appreciation of him and his friendship for the South appear in the notice of his passing taken by the *Messenger* in those days of immediate and absorbing trouble. In the February (1864) number, the great novelist's death was announced in a page and a half editorial. In the March number nearly four pages were given to an essay by Capt. W. Gordon McCabe who found time to write it in the midst of his arduous labors as a gallant officer in Lee's Army. The April number contained a two page " In Memoriam " by Dickens, reprinted from the *Cornhill Magazine,* of which Thackeray had been the founder.

The hall in which Thackeray lectured in the Athenæum was adorned with paintings presented to it by Mr. Conway Robinson who brought them from London for that purpose. He also selected when there many choice books for the two public library rooms provided in the Athenæum building by the City Council. These two rooms with their collections, were known as the City Library and the Historical Library. The Virginia Historical Society met at the Athenæum, and in one of the smaller rooms of this centre of culture Alexander Galt the sculptor had his studio where his " Bacchante ", " Psyche " and other works were on exhibition. In April and in December, 1853, courses of lectures by leading lecturers of America and Europe were delivered at the Athenæum.

JOSEPH JEFFERSON. IN 1910, IN VALENTINE'S STUDIO, LOOKING AT A BUST OF
HIS FRIEND EDWIN BOOTH

The bust was made from life in this studio in 1857, when Booth was twenty-five years old and
Valentine twenty.   Courtesy of Mr. Valentine

ANDROMACHE AND ASTYNAX
Marble group by Edward V. Valentine.   Courtesy of Mr. Valentine

IN VALENTINE'S STUDIO
Bust of Jefferson Davis in foreground

CHAPTER XXI

THE THEATRE

RICHMOND's *Noctes Ambrosianæ* were not confined to literary lectures. A few days before Christmas, 1850, when holiday spirit filled the air, Virginia's Capital took into its warm heart Jenny Lind and her enthralling voice, described by one of the fortunates who heard it as " exquisitely soft, like the music of pearls in a golden basin." For her one concert Marshall Theatre at Broad and Seventh Streets was sold out at auction—the seats bringing from $8 to $105 apiece.

To this old Marshall Theatre (named for John Marshall who, by the way, dearly loved a good play) came the leading actors of the time—including the Booths and lovable Joe Jefferson. In 1857, Jefferson was manager of the theatre as well as member of a stock company in which he played " Rip Van Winkle " and other rôles. He lived with his family at Swan Tavern (where another distinguished Jefferson had once been a familiar figure) and was popular in society. He believed that he would become better known as a painter than as an actor and affiliated with artists. In Richmond one of his favorite haunts was the studio of the twenty-year-old sculptor, Edward V. Valentine, in whom both he and the young Edwin Booth found a kindred spirit. An interesting memorial of this three cornered friendship (which continued throughout the lives of both actors and is today affectionately remembered by the venerable sculptor), is a photograph taken in the studio during Jefferson's last visit to Richmond, showing him as an old man gazing at a bust of Booth which " Ned " Valentine had made in 1857.

When in Richmond during his later life Jefferson used to recall both sad and happy memories of old days at the " Swan." One night when he was living there he was about to appear as " Touchstone ", in " As You Like It ", when a message came for him which made him instantly turn his cap and bells over to an understudy and hasten away to the death-bed of his infant son, Joseph, Jr.

Booth, in those days, once played thirteen consecutive nights at the Marshall theatre. Perhaps it was then that he fell in love with Mary Devlin, a young actress of Jefferson's stock company, who became his adored wife.

Throughout the dark days of Civil War the theatre helped those who could raise the small fee then asked for admission, to forget.

CHAPTER XXII

"TIPPECANOE AND TYLER TOO"

WHATEVER happens or does not happen in Virginia's capital interest in politics is always lively. In 1840 there was bitter war of words between the Whigs and the Democrats, as the old Republicans were calling themselves. Richmond had become a Whig strong-hold and the party's nomination of Gen. William H. Harrison (born at "Berkeley", on James River, a few miles below Richmond) for President of the United States, and John Tyler, of "Greenway Court", in the same county, for Vice-President, was greeted with enthusiasm. Both candidates had been familiar figures in Richmond in their youth and Tyler had lived there as Governor of Virginia. Henry Clay, the great Whig leader, who was also a native of the neighborhood, had been a member of Chancellor Wythe's law school and knew everybody in town, came from Kentucky to take part in the campaigning and the Whigs had the time of their lives. General Harrison's victory over the Indians of the Northwest in 1811 had won for him the soubriquet of "Old Tippecanoe." So "Tippecanoe and Tyler Too" became the party slogan. As reminders of Harrison's pioneer experiences, buildings in which to hold campaign meetings took the form of log-cabins, decorated with coon skins, and sprouted up in every part of the country where Whig sentiment existed. On the site of the Eagle Hotel (which had been burned), Richmonders built such a cabin to hold 3000 persons, and night after night local and visiting orators almost raised its roof. Among home Whigs who played leading parts in these log-cabin scenes were Raleigh Travers Daniel, James Lyons, Wyndham Robertson, Benjamin Watkins Leigh, Sydney S. Baxter, William H. McFarland, Robert C. Standard, and John Minor Botts. One wet night when the orator was William C. Preston, of South Carolina, celebrated for his dramatic power and fascination on the platform, hundreds who could not get inside stood out in the rain, seeing and hearing what they could through windows and crevices between the logs.

The interest taken in the campaign by all sorts and conditions of people is illustrated by a comical story. A Whig delegation from Culpeper County with coon skin decorated log-cabin, on wheels, attended a meeting in Richmond and marched into Capitol Square. One of the visitors recognized in the crowd which gathered around the Cabin his young cousin, William B. Wooldridge (in after years the gallant Colonel of the 4th Virginia Cavalry, C. S. A., and the teller of this story), whom he asked to hold the Culpeper flag, while the delegates sought refreshment at a tavern. Immediately afterward a thief was caught picking a pocket and was marched off to jail, followed by a throng, including the boy proudly carrying the Culpeper flag, with its device of a coiled rattlesnake and legend: "Don't tread on me." When the jail was reached the pick-pocket asked the constable to give him a few minutes and mounting a box proceeded to make a fiery "Tippecanoe and Tyler Too" speech.

And now appears what looks like the first sign of division in political parties in regard to "wetness" or "dryness." Behold a Temperance Society is born in Richmond whose pledge seems to presage the death knell of the free punch-bowl at the Governor's Mansion. "We will not use intoxicating liquor as a beverage during the session of the Legislature of Virginia", wisely, but doubtless sadly in many cases, promise its members. *Man was made to mourn.*

With the ringing in of a new leap year (which is, of course, the year for another presidential election), politics run high again. Who shall be elected—Clay or Polk? Bitterer than ever grows the contention. Even the voteless sex are arrayed on one side or the other, and the " Whig ladies " are busy collecting funds for a statue to their idol for Capitol Square. But this is not to be one of the times when Virginia will be mother of a president. . . .

News comes that war with Mexico is declared. Again history repeats itself. Again Richmond mothers, wives and sweethearts send their boys off to serve their country on the battle field. Three companies of volunteers go to Old Point, where they will take ship for Mexico, and a great crowd gathers at the wharf to bid the soldiers goodbye. Again war is the all absorbing topic. Again women knit and sew for soldiers while they watch and wait for letters and newspapers. When news of the victory of Vera Cruz comes everybody runs out to see the Fayette Artillery parade and follows them to Gamble's Hill—the Hill of the Grey Cross—where they unfurl a new flag and fire a salute.

In the midst of wartimes a shipload of clothing and groceries is sent direct from sympathetic Richmond Town to famine-stricken Ireland, and later, a meeting is held in Odd Fellows Hall in the interest of Irish freedom.

CHAPTER XXIII

DUELING

AND in the midst of wartimes political discussion went on and on. Should slavery be abolished? If so how could it be accomplished? Ah, this was the hardest of all nuts to crack.

On February 24, 1846, Thomas Ritchie, Jr., of the *Enquirer,* received from John Hampden Pleasants of the *Whig,* with whom he had a violent quarrel, a challenge to meet him on the Manchester side of the river, next morning at sunrise—" armed with sidearms, without rifle, shotgun or musket " and " accompanied by two friends similarly armed." Ritchie replied protesting against the challenge as " not in the form justified by men of honor, and to great extent upheld by public opinion ", and furthermore, " savage, sanguinary, and revolting to the taste and judgment . . . of every man in the community." But concluding: " I shall be on the ground mentioned at sunrise."

His protest bears witness to the tyranny of public opinion which made it impossible for a man to decline a challenge. In the peaceful, frosty, February dawn the antagonists met and, after a bloody encounter with dirks, sword-canes and pistols, Pleasants, the idol of his party and of a host of friends, was borne from the field mortally wounded.

There continued to be occasional duels in Richmond until the eighteen-eighties when laws having utterly failed to put an end to the practice, the powerful remedy of ridicule came to the rescue, and the " affair of honor " was simply laughed out of existence.

DUELING

One of the most sensational duels in the city's history —and the last to prove fatal—was over a statuesque, golden-haired "Mary." Among her many devoted cavaliers were Page McCarty, clever editor, and his chum, John B. Mordecai, kinsman of the author of *Richmond in By-Gone Days*. At a ball on a spring night of 1878, at which all Richmond society was present, she showed Mordecai such marked favor and McCarty such conspicuous indifference, that the editor soon left the ballroom in a rage. Subscribers to the *Richmond Enquirer*, unfolding their papers next morning, were regaled with this poetical tribute to "The First Figure in the German":

> "When Mary's queenly form I press,
>   In Strauss's latest waltz,
> I would as well her lips caress,
>   Although those lips were false.
> For still with fire love tips his dart
>   And kindles up anew
> The flame which once consumed my heart,
>   When those dear lips were true."

Gossip buzzed. There was no doubt about the identity of "Mary"—the bright, particular star of the Richmond German—and the anonymous rhymes were at once attributed to her slighted lover. The wrathful Mordecai charged him with their authorship and later sent him a challenge. A remote and gruesomely suggestive spot was the scene of the meeting at sunset, on the ninth of May. It was back of Oakwood cemetery! The seconds and surgeons on both sides were men of social prominence. They were Col. W. B. Tabb, John S. Meredith and Dr. J. S. D. Cullen—for McCarty—and William L. Royall, William R. Trigg and Dr. Hunter McGuire—for Mordecai. The weapons were Colts, navy revolvers with army balls, at ten paces.

The antagonists—each twenty-seven years old—grimly faced each other and two shots rang out. No harm was done, but their pistols were still raised—with determined aim this time. Again two shots rang out. Both young lovers fell and quickly the green grass bloomed red with their life-blood. While the surgeons were binding up their wounds the police arrived and placed the whole party under arrest. The surgeons were excused on their plea that they had no part in the affair except to give professional aid. The duelists and their seconds were bailed. Mordecai's death (after five days) threw the city into a fever of excitement. McCarty and the seconds were again placed under arrest. McCarty was too ill from his wound to be removed to prison and was kept under guard at his home, while the seconds were taken to jail and kept there for more than two months, when they were released on bail. McCarty was not well enough to stand trial until the following January, when he was convicted of manslaughter, fined $500 (which was paid) and sentenced to prison. In February he was pardoned on account of his physical condition.

In 1858 Richmond's taste for pageantry was gratified in unique fashion. The state legislature of that year had appropriated $2,000 for bringing to Virginia the body of President Monroe, who had died in New York and been buried there. He had died on July 4th, and his home-coming, twenty-seven years afterward, was made a Fourth of July celebration. The casket escorted by a regiment of New York volunteers was taken by steamer to Richmond. There it was met by two regiments of Virginia volunteers and the Richmond military, and was borne by pall-bearers appointed by the Governor to a hearse drawn by six snow-white horses, attended by six negro grooms, in white uniforms. The chief marshal for the occasion and his six assistants were mounted on spirited horses and clad in white uniforms with black sashes. All Richmond looked on in silent admiration. Flags were

PRESIDENTS' HILL, HOLLYWOOD CEMETERY

Tombs of President James Monroe (centre) and John Tyler (left), and of Commodore Mathew F. Maury
and John Y. Mason.

at half mast. "Boom—Boom—Boom," said the minute guns and tolling church bells added a more solemn note still to the out-door drama of that long-ago summer's day. Softly the band began to play a dirge. Slowly the procession moved through town to Hollywood Cemetery on one of whose green hills had been erected—within a cage-like wrought-iron enclosure—a marble sarcophagus. In this the pall-bearers placed their burden.

After the ceremonies the Virginia military escorted the New York regiment to a banquet at Gallego Mills. At night Capitol Square was illuminated, and again the soldiers were feasted.

In October of the following year the body of John Y. Mason, United States Minister to France, who had died in Paris, was laid to rest near that of Monroe, and a little more than two years later President John Tyler, who died in Richmond, found a last resting place in Hollywood, on this same hillock—now known as "Presidents' Hill"—on top of which also sleeps the great "pathfinder of the seas," Commodore Matthew F. Maury.

PART VI

THE WAR BETWEEN THE STATES AND RECONSTRUCTION

(1859-1870)

CHAPTER XXIV

RICHMOND AND THE JOHN BROWN RAID

OCTOBER, 1859, found Richmond in a state of peaceful activity. The population had reached nearly 38,000. Many new business ventures were being projected, and educational, religious and philanthropic works going ahead. During the year much company had enabled the people to indulge their social instincts. In May the Baptist General Association of Virginia had met in the First Baptist Church. Later in the same month the city, already bright with buttercups and newly put on verdure, blossomed gallantly with gold braid, long white plumes and embroidered sashes, when it entertained for three days the Knights Templar of Massachusetts and Rhode Island. And now when autumn's sun shone on the many-colored trees of hilltops beyond the city, and hill and dale within it, until it seemed that upon it " a rainbow from the firmament had surely fallen ", the General Convention of the Episcopal Church in America was, for the first time, having its three weeks' session in Virginia—at (the then new) St. Paul's Church, opposite Capitol Square. Bishops, clergy and laymen from all over the Union filled every chink in Richmond's hospitable homes. The " comfortable, friendly, cheery little town " was fragrant with cake and bread-baking, coffee-roasting and chicken-frying, and noisy with laughter and chatter. Morning, noon and night the bell in the lofty steeple rang and from the open windows sounds of psalm-chanting and hymn-singing floated out to the streets.

On such a scene of peace-on-earth fell, on October

17th, in the form of a telegram to Governor Wise, a thunderbolt out of season.

More picturesque even, than The Falls of James River is Harper's Ferry, on the western border of the present State of Virginia, where, rising abruptly opposite each other, Virginia Heights and Maryland Heights look down upon the meeting of two rivers. Through this gate-beautiful of Nature's building the Kansas fanatic, John Brown encouraged by certain Northern abolitionists, and followed by his band of raiders, had passed and seized the United States Arsenal with the design of freeing the slaves and equipping them with arms.

Richmond flamed with excitement. Nobody knew what death, destruction and chaos might be the result of such a plot. Governor Wise after telegraphing orders to the cavalry and infantry companies in the neighborhood of the trouble, left by the earliest train possible— taking with him some of the Richmond military. Of course a telegram had been sent from Harper's Ferry to President Buchanan, at Washington. He sent to the scene a battalion of marines commanded by Col. Robert E. Lee, who with his Aide, Lieut. J. E. B. Stuart, took charge of the situation and (with some bloodshed on each side) captured the Arsenal. John Brown was later tried and hanged. Contrary to his expectations, no slaves had joined his raid (though a few free negroes had); but after it no such thing as lying down in peace was possible in Richmond, or elsewhere in the South.

For years North and South had been moving—slowly but surely—toward a crisis, and more—toward a conflagration, for which each section was piling up fagots— piling up fagots. Richmond had been a battleground for the earliest wars between white men and red men which gave the Anglo-Saxon race a foothold on American soil.

THE WAR RESIDENCE OF GENERAL LEE
Now the home of the Virginia Historical Society

RICHMOND AND THE JOHN BROWN RAID

Richmond had done its bit to save America for Americans in the wars of the Revolution and 1812, and in the war with Mexico. Soon Richmond was to become the centre of an amphitheatre about which would charge the four dread Horsemen—War, Pestilence, Famine, Death. North and South piled up the fagots. John Brown had applied the match. Immediately after his " raid " Virginia's Capital began busily preparing for war—if war should come. New military companies were organized. The students of Richmond College formed themselves into one. Two hundred and fifty odd Southern boys studying medicine in Philadelphia came home and entered the Medical College of Virginia. They were met by the home students, the military and many citizens, and escorted to Capitol Square where there was a demonstration in their honor.

Yet Richmond was prospering. Progress and preparations for possible war went side by side. Early in the new year the first steam fire engine ever seen in Richmond was built there for the Russian Government, and shipped —after home-folk had proudly inspected it and it had been exhibited in Washington, Baltimore, Philadelphia and New York. The Henry Clay statue unveiling was a gala occasion when there was a great banquet for home and visiting Whigs.

The Richmond and York River Railroad was nearing completion. The Richmond and Lynchburg Road was about to be started and the Street Railway would soon have horse cars running from Rocketts to Brook Road. Many houses were building. The hopeful sounds of hammer and saw were heard from sun-up to sundown, and mingling with them, the mellow voices of care-free negroes joking and laughing and singing as they worked, and the thinner tones of the white foremen as they cracked jokes after their fashion, whistled any tune that happened to run in their heads from a camp meeting melody to one learned from some darkie's flute or fiddle, or discussed politics—for 1860 was presidential election year, remember. Occasionally all other sounds were drowned by the rattle of a passing cart-load of bricks or the lusty cry of a huckster with his mule and covered cart: " F-e-e-sh, Fe-e-sh," or " Swe-e-e-t watermillions—Green rind, red meat, full of juice and so-o-o sweet ", or other produce according to season. The doctor's gig, my lady's carriage, the slow-moving funeral hack, the lumbering dray, each added its distinct note to the deafening chorus of traffic over cobblestones of the few business streets, or the almost soundless rhythm in the residence streets—innocent of paving, dirty and dusty, but blissfully quiet.

Sometimes all other sights and sounds were blotted out by interest (with little realization of its significance) in a parade of one of the new military companies on its way to drill. And with so many new enterprises going forward, the old Armory was aroused from its slumber and equipped with improved machinery for the manufacture of muskets and other arms. Many of those who were to use them were already learning the manual in Richmond and other places. Many others were boys playing in the streets with no dream of the weariness of long marches on empty stomachs, in ragged shoes or no shoes at all, of the thirst a bleeding wound could create or the anguish of amputation without anæsthetics.

On Saturday, October 6, 1860, the ordinary routine was agreeably broken by a visit of the Prince of Wales— many years later to be King Edward VII, of England. He arrived in Richmond with his suite, on a special train decorated with British and American colors, spent the night at the " Ballard House " and was given a banquet at the " Exchange." On Sunday he heard Doctor

IN THE OLD MARKET

SELLING A WATERMELON

THE WHOLESALE PRODUCE DISTRICT IN THE EIGHTEEN-NINETIES

IN A TOBACCO FACTORY

Minnigerode preach at St. Paul's, visited St. John's and Hollywood, and on Monday morning—from the rear platform of his train, waved goodbye to the whole of Richmond, gathered at the station to see him off. Later in the month was held Virginia's most successful Agricultural Fair, so far. The crowds who in the daytime visited the Fair grounds (the present Monroe Park) had plenty of entertainment at night, for Adelina Patti—then a girl playing with dolls—sang three nights at Corinthian Hall, Joe Jefferson was appearing at Marshall Theatre and the Negro pianist " Blind Tom " was playing at the African Church. But the election was rapidly approaching and the minute the Fair was over the town was absorbed in politics again.

CHAPTER XXV

WAR BEGINS

NIGHT after night political speeches packed the African Church and every other available auditorium. Night after night torchlight processions led by brass bands lit up the streets. The most vital and exciting subject discussed was that of relations between North and South—relations resulting chiefly from inability of each section to understand the other. Richmond was filled with men devoted to the Union which their fathers had so large a part in constructing—to which Virginia had given the orator whose voice had hastened the Revolution into being, the author of the Declaration of Independence, the expounder of the Constitution, seven of the fifteen Presidents, and other builders of the nation, many of whom had learned their first lessons in statecraft in Richmond's small, pillared capitol and had been (as Governors of Virginia or members of the Assembly and Conventions) residents of Richmond and familiar figures in its homes and streets. Yes, Richmond was devoted to the Union and had been shocked when Massachusetts twice in former times had threatened to secede—though believing that she would be within her rights in so doing if she should see fit. For Richmond believed the Union which it loved to be composed of independent states with right to solve their own problems. The problem regarded with greatest anxiety by leaders of thought in Virginia and other southern states was the Negro. Virginia had declared by Act of Assembly, one year before Richmond became its capital, that "From and after the passing of this Act no slaves shall hereafter be imported into this commonwealth by sea or land, nor shall any slaves so imported be sold or bought by any person whatsoever." Yet slaves were already there in numbers which the natural increase of a race of such fecundity was adding to by leaps and bounds. All intelligent advocates of freeing them felt that it would have to be done gradually—a few at a time. These servants (Virginians rarely used the word slave) were dependent not only for food, raiment and shelter, but for guidance, upon their masters. What would become of them if turned loose upon the community? What would become of the community subject to the depredations certain to follow? Many Virginia masters directed in their wills that their slaves be freed—generally, a few at a time. Many others saw differently. They had been born in a section where slavery had long existed. They believed in making the best of a difficult condition. Others still —among them—devout Christians—took slavery as a matter of course. They believed that it was the plan of the Creator for the black race to serve the white—the white to be providers for and counsellors of the black. A very great number were convinced that disapproval of slavery in the northern states had its origin in the undesirability of slave labor for northern industries and climate, increased by jealousy of the prosperity it might bring to cotton and other agricultural districts of the South. All believed that the South would solve her problem in the course of time, and resented dictation or coercion from sections unfamiliar with that problem.

The North, excited by exaggerated pictures of the evils of slavery painted by writers and speakers with little or no first-hand knowledge of the subject, forgetting that Washington, Marshall and many other southerners of as conspicuous rectitude were masters of slaves, believed it to be its duty to reform the wicked slave-holding states —a holier-than-thou attitude most irritating to the South. North and South—each with honest convictions—were looking at opposite sides of a shield—each, by reason of what it saw there, blindly and bitterly impaling the other. In Richmond, as in other cities, the great bulk of the population owned no slaves. The well-to-do owned only enough to supply their houses with servants and their business places with " hands ", porters, janitors and the like, with the exception of gentlemen who kept up country estates as well as city homes.

Election day at last! After it men looked grave and spoke apprehensively in Richmond—as throughout the South. They feared that the election of a President of the United States without a single electoral vote from a southern state—a solid North for Abraham Lincoln, a solid South against him—would precipitate war and divide the Union. The South was not against the man personally. Of him it knew little. But though the Republican platform asserted " the right of each state to order and control its domestic institutions according to its own judgment exclusively ", the Capital of Virginia and the whole South saw the choice of the Republican candidate as President, not as an election by the people, for the people, but an election by one section of the people out of sympathy with and ignorant of the problems of the other, of a man of its own way of thinking and its own lack of knowledge of southern conditions to be President over the whole people.

South Carolina had threatened to secede if the Republican candidate should be elected and hard upon the heels of the election came to Richmond the news that South Carolina had seceded and was calling for the establishment of a Southern Confederacy. Two days after Christmas a meeting of Richmond citizens which crowded the

African Church adopted a resolution calling for a State Convention to determine Virginia's rights within the Union or out of it, disapproving of any move toward coercion of seceding states and discouraging a beginning of hostilities of any seceding state before the formation of a Southern Confederacy.

Richmond's prosperity stopped like a clock which had had a jolt, and financial panic followed. The cheerful chorus of men singing at their work to the accompaniment of hammer and saw and mill whistle and factory wheel, was stilled—and the stillness was oppressive. A bitter cold winter had set in and the eyes of the unemployed held the anguished question: Where are we to find bread for our children? In the capital that had been so cheerful and gay the stage was set for the most tragic drama of all, and Governor Letcher appointed January 4th as a day of fasting and prayer. On January 19th, the Virginia Legislature, sitting in the Capitol, adopted resolutions inviting all of the states—slave-holding or free—to join Virginia in sending Commissioners to Washington on February 4th, for a Peace Conference which should make plans to avert war and save the Union. Ex-President John Tyler, William C. Rives, John W. Brockenbrough, George W. Summers and James A. Seddon were named as delegates to the conference from Virginia and John Robertson was chosen to visit the other states and urge them to appoint Commissioners. South Carolina declined because she had already seceded, had invited other Southern States to meet her in Convention in Montgomery, Alabama, and some of them had accepted. Virginia's Peace Conference met in Washington with thirteen Northern and seven Southern states represented —but it was too late. While it was in session a convention of six Southern States at Montgomery, Alabama, was in session too, and organized the Southern Confederacy, with Jefferson Davis as President and Alexander H. Stephens, Vice-President. On February 13th, the State Convention called for by the people of Richmond during Christmas week (and authorized by the Legislature), the Convention soon to pass into history as the Virginia Secession Convention, held its first session, with John Janney, of Loudoun County, as President and John L. Eubank, of Richmond, Secretary. It met in the Capitol (in the Hall of the House of Delegates), except when the Assembly was in session, when it used Mechanic's Hall. In either hall, all available space was crowded by men and women listening anxiously to argument as to what Virginia's course should be, while outside, ominous preparations went steadily, steadily on. At night the people swarmed to meetings held by secessionists impatient for Virginia to commit herself, and by their opponents pleading for preservation of the Union.

The Convention was still in session when March 4th arrived and the people crowded about the bulletin boards to read reports of President Lincoln's inauguration flying over telegraph wires. It was still in session on April 12th, when news came of the bombardment of Fort Sumter, in Charleston Harbor, by Confederate troops, and its surrender by its Federal Commandant. Alas, America! Civil War was a fact! Drunk with enthusiasm kindled by this first victory of Southern arms, Richmond people poured cheering into the streets. Some of them set a Confederate flag fluttering from the top of the Capitol. An artillery salute was fired. It is written (in the diary of young William S. White a member of the newly formed Richmond Howitzers): "Nightfall, instead of quieting the excitement, seemed if possible, to add fresh fuel to the flame. The crowded streets and wild shouts of the people, together with the lurid glare of an hundred tar-barrels, torches steeped in rosin, and rockets whirling high above the houses, presented a spectacle rarely witnessed by our somewhat apathetic people of Richmond."

Were these people moved by desire to preserve slavery? Most of them had never owned, never expected to own a slave.

On that same historic April day, the Convention sent William Ballard Preston, Alexander H. H. Stuart and George Randolph to Washington, to ask the President what his attitude toward the seceding states would be. He replied (quoting his inaugural address): "The power confided in me will be used to hold, occupy and possess the property and places belonging to the government, and to collect the duties and imports; but beyond what is necessary for these objects there will be no invasion, no using of force against or among the people anywhere." Before the Commissioners could present this answer to the Convention, eagerly awaiting it in Richmond, President Lincoln had called for 75,000 troops to reduce the seceding states, and asked Virginia for her quota. Governor Letcher declined to send a man from Virginia to make war on her sister states of the South. For once, party differences were forgotten in Richmond. People of every shade of opinion were bound together in a brotherhood to protect the rights of Southern States and defend Southern homes against an invading army. Virginia recognized in the President's call for troops a declaration of war. "The peacefulness and quiet of Richmond had now" (in the words of one who was there), "become a tradition. Fierce agitation replaced the old tranquillity and in the streets, the hotels, the drawing-rooms, nothing was heard but hot discussion. Men's pulses were feverish. Neighbors of opposite sides scowled fiercely at each other.

Young ladies wore Southern colors and would turn their backs upon an admirer who was not for secession."

The cockade of South Carolina was everywhere worn. Everything, even the social life of young folk, centred around the Capitol where the Convention was in session. It is written that "It was the habit of the young ladies to promenade with their gallants in the Capitol Square, in the evening, and enjoy the strains of a fine band stationed on a rostrum opposite the City Hall" and overlooking the Square.

The seriousness of the situation was reflected in the countenances and bearing of the Convention and in the grave debate which showed that many members who had been most earnest advocates of preserving the Union so long as it could be preserved with peace, were heart and soul with the South now that war was unavoidable. The spectators who had packed the hall were turned out and the Convention went into secret session, but instead of going home the people swarmed in the Square, waiting with intense anxiety to hear the fate of Virginia which they knew hung on the words that were being spoken within that building of many happenings, where the most solemn scene in Richmond's drama was there being enacted. On April 17th, the final vote was taken and the Ordinance of Secession passed by 103 to 43 votes. The announcement made on the next morning was received with wildest joy by the people. The flag of the newly formed Southern Confederacy was run up on the staff on the roof of the Capitol. The crowd in the Square saluted it with cheers. The Custom House was taken in charge by military officers of the state and preparations to provide barracks for soldiers and commissary stores for their support begun.

On the next night Richmond again blazed with bonfires and fireworks and ten thousand hurrahing men and boys carried torches and transparencies in the longest and most enthusiastic torchlight procession the city had ever seen—to celebrate Virginia's secession from the Union of which this, her capital had been a stronghold.

The invading army was already on its march southward, and Richmond soldier companies were ready for orders to " Fall in " at a moment's notice. On Sunday, April 21st, services were going on in the churches and chatter of children, on their way home from Sunday school, sweet and clean in their Sunday clothes, mingled pleasantly with bird flutings and the distant roar of the falls floating in at windows opened to the spring morning. Suddenly, the bell in the Capitol tower sounded—! One —two—three—silence. And again, one—two—three— silence. It was the signal agreed upon—the first command of the war! Immediately churches were emptied. The soldiers were the first to hurry out and to hear that the big United States steamer *Pawnee*—after having done great damage to Norfolk Navy Yard—was on its way up James River to bombard and capture Richmond. " With a shout the soldiers rushed to their *rendezvous.*" The artillery and infantry were marched down either side of the river, the Governor's guard and cavalry sent out to reconnoitre. The remainder of the inhabitants—men, women, children—swarmed upon the bluffs overlooking the river to see the battle. But there was no battle. Hours passed and it finally developed that the visit of the *Pawnee* was a false alarm. " Pawnee Sunday " and the " Pawnee War " were soon subjects of merriment, but they stimulated enlistment and preparation for real war.

CHAPTER XXVI

ENTER ROBERT E. LEE

THE serious problem confronting "honest John" Letcher was choice of the right man to command Virginia's troops. Soon his thoughts fixed themselves upon Colonel Robert E. Lee, who represented all that birth and breeding could give toward making a gentleman, with the best that West Point training and the experience his brilliant record in the Mexican War could add in making a soldier and an officer. Colonel Lee, feeling that " though opposed to secession and deprecating war " he could take no part in an invasion of the Southern States ", had tendered General Scott his resignation as an officer in the United States Army (which he probably could have commanded if he had elected to remain in it) and returned to his home and family at " Arlington." At " Arlington " from whose portico he had so often looked with pride upon fair Washington—a mile away —Capital of the Union he had loved and fought for! Before deciding on his next step he would have a few days of domestic peace at " Arlington " whose stately groves and fruitful fields were at the height of spirit-resting beauty. At " Arlington ", so soon to lock its doors upon him—to be part of the price he would pay for loyalty to his native state and his South. It was at " Arlington " that " honest John's " invitation reached Robert E. Lee, and on Monday following " Pawnee Sunday " he arrived in Richmond. At stations all along the road he had been sped on his way by cheering crowds and at Central Depot he found a welcoming multitude. He was not only believed to be the prize of the United States

THE CONFEDERATE MEMORIAL INSTITUTE (BATTLE ABBEY)
Copyright. Courtesy of the Confederate Memorial Institute

GROUP OF CONFEDERATE GENERALS
Detail from Fresco by Hoffbauer, in the "Battle Abbey"
Copyright. Courtesy of the Confederate Memorial Institute

MARSHAL FOCH AND CONFEDERATE VETERANS ON THE SPOT WHERE LEE PLANNED
THE "SEVEN DAYS BATTLES"
Armistice Day, 1921

CARING FOR THE WOUNDED
Fresco in "Battle Abbey"
Copyright.   Courtesy of the Confederate Memorial Institute

Army, but there was something about this handsome, erect but not very tall, gentle, human, unostentatious man unanimously described by those who knew him as " grandeur." Mary Johnston in her book, *Cease Firing,* introduces him dramatically with : " One rode ahead on a grey horse. Noble of form and noble of face, simple and courteous he came ... and grandeur came with him." An old, old lady who was his neighbor in Richmond during the war, asked to describe him said : " He had a look of grandeur. A man of a younger generation who (as a Virginia Military Institute student) saw him constantly in his after-the-war home, at Lexington said : " He was modest, approachable, gentle, indulging in flashes of quiet humor, but there was something about him which can only be expressed by the word grandeur."

At the Spotswood Hotel he found another great crowd of people eager to greet him. They clamored for a speech and he delighted them with a few earnest words.

On the same day Governor Letcher announced to the Secession Convention still sitting in the Capitol that (with their consent) he would appoint Colonel Lee commander of Virginia's military and naval forces. Next day, as the hand of the clock in the historic Hall of the House pointed to 12 there was a lull in the proceedings of the Convention. The door had opened and the man who moved modestly, but within an aura of grandeur, stood on its threshold, " on the arm " of Major Marmaduke Johnson. As one man, the Convention arose to its feet. Half way up the aisle Major Johnson, pausing, said : " Mr. President, I have the honor to present to you and to the Convention Major General Lee." Mr. Janney acknowledged the introduction eloquently. General Lee replied : " Mr. President and Gentlemen of the Convention—Profoundly impressed with the solemnity of the occasion, for which I must say I was unprepared, I accept the position assigned me by your partiality. I would have much preferred had the choice fallen upon an abler man. Trusting in Almighty God, an approving conscience and the aid of my fellow citizens, I devote myself to the service of my native State, in whose behalf alone will I ever again draw my sword."

To say that this great soldier was unsheathing his sword to preserve the institution of slavery would be absurd. The only slaves he had ever owned were a few inherited from his mother and he had freed them long before the war. In 1856 he had declared slavery to be " a greater evil to the white than to the black race ", adding, " while my feelings are strongly enlisted in behalf of the latter, my sympathies are strongly for the former." His wife was the daughter of Martha Washington's grandson, George Washington Parke Custis, who ordered in his will that his slaves be freed within five years. In 1862, General Lee, as executor, left his army long enough to carry out this direction of his father-in-law.

CHAPTER XXVII
ENTER JEFFERSON DAVIS

On April 27, 1861, the Convention invited President Jefferson to make Richmond the seat of his government. The invitation was accepted by the Provisional Congress at Montgomery. On May 29th, the President arrived in Richmond, and the capital of Virginia became the capital of the Confederacy. The City Council had bought a worthy White House (the Brockenbrough Mansion, in the " Court End " of town), then the home of Mr. James A. Seddon and now the Confederate Museum. The Committee from the Provisional Congress held that the Confederacy, and no one city, should provide the President's house, and had the city reimbursed.

Richmond's newest citizen had a national reputation as one of the brilliant public men of his time. He, too, was a West Pointer and a distinguished veteran of the Mexican War. He had represented Mississippi in House and Senate and had been Secretary of War during Pierce's administration. Later he had returned to his seat in the Senate, where he remained until the secession of Mississippi, when he resigned and made his way back to his home in Dixie. He had not been an extreme secessionist, and his election was regarded as an attempt to meet the wishes of the conservative group of southerners. Curiously, the President in Washington and the President in Richmond were strikingly alike in person. Both were born in the year 1808, and in the same State—Kentucky. But—during early childhood Lincoln was taken by his parents to Indiana; Davis to Mississippi. So it is probable that the attitude of these two men of destiny toward a question which was temporarily splitting the Union in two, and the part taken by each in deciding it, was largely a matter of geography. Suppose when the boys left Kentucky little Abe Lincoln had gone to Mississippi and been cuddled in the soft arms of a black mammy, and little Jeff Davis had gone to Indiana to be fed on tales of the mal-treatment of poor darkies by ogrous Southern masters? Well, suppose the moon were really made of green cheese!

President Davis was received with joy by the people who, over and over again, crowded about and stopped his carriage to shake his hand as he passed through the streets to Spotswood Hotel, where he, like General Lee, had to speak a few words to them to satisfy their clamor.

Now Virginia's State House becomes the Capitol of the Confederacy—the meeting place of the Confederate Congress. The President's office was in the Custom House, on Main Street, the War Department in Mechanic's Hall on Ninth and Franklin, the Patent Office in Goddin's Building at Bank and Eleventh Streets. And now cap-ture of Richmond on the James becomes the chief object of the Government at Washington. " On to Richmond " shout the armies of the North on the march to attack Vir-ginia's Capital, and " On to Richmond " answer the armies of the South on the march to defend it. Hired negro labor-ers swing their picks throwing up barriers against the forces coming to free their race. Chanting of their " spirit-ual " melodies keeps time with the rhythmic movement of their bodies. Another sound breaks on the air. A train has come in bringing a company of rosy-cheeked, bright-eyed grey-clad boys, who are marching through town with fife and drum. People in the streets are clapping and yell-ing the weird " Ah-e-e-e, ah-e-e-e," to become known as the " Rebel yell." The negro laborers break off in the middle of some such song as:

" There were ten virgins when the Bridegroom come," and take up the air the fife is playing—supplying the words:

    " Dixie lan' whar I was born in,
    Early on one frosty mornin',
    Ahway, Ahway, Ahway down souf in Dixie!"

White House of the Confederacy

THE CONFEDERACY, NOW THE CONFEDERATE MUSEUM

ing by Virginia A. Garber, by courtesy of the artist

STAIRWAY IN THE WHITE HOUSE OF THE CONFEDERACY, NOW THE
CONFEDERATE MUSEUM

From a drawing by Virginia A. Garber, by courtesy of the artist

ENTER JEFFERSON DAVIS

The whole town was busy with preparation for the conflict which everybody in it felt certain would soon be over, with victory for the Confederacy. Belle Isle Iron Works, Tredegar Iron Works, and the Armory were manufacturing munitions; women made uniforms and tents; the Council and business men raised money to equip the volunteers who crowd to recruiting stations, and also to provide for the families of men whose only business now must be war, and to care for those who would be brought back sick and wounded. Children played soldier in the streets—brandishing broom-stick guns with avowed intention to " shoot all the Yankees." One little fellow soon to be fatherless closed his prayer at his mother's knee with : " Please God keep the Confederate flag on top of the Capitol." All trains brought troops from some part of Virginia or from other Southern states, who were marched to the camps—one at the Fair Grounds (the present Monroe Park), one at Richmond College, one at Howard's Grove (on Mechanicsville turnpike), one on Chimborazo Hill. Indeed, the whole town seemed to have suddenly turned into a military encampment.

Inclination would draw a veil of forgetfulness over the hatred that was breeding in Richmond against the North and in the North against Richmond, but such a veil would give history the lie, and history must be " the light of truth." Today, in five National Cemeteries in and about Richmond tens of thousands of tiny stone markers dot the grass above the ashes of those who surrounded the town in what many of them conscientiously believed to be a holy cause, and in Richmond's own cemeteries similar bits of stone mark the spots where sleep the city's devoted defenders. Fifty-odd years after the struggle, interested tourists or sorrowful pilgrims are constantly visiting these pitiful graves. Annually, they are watered

171

with tears and decorated with flowers. Each one of them represents a tragic break in some home circle of long ago—North or South.

But more pathetic than the thought of their mangled young bodies—of their snuffed out lives, is that of the hate that brought these brave lads at grips. To kill one another, men must hate. To the North all Southern soldiers were " damn Rebels ", in Richmond and throughout the Confederacy all Northerners were " damn Yankees."

To add fuel to the fires of hatred of Yankees which the war itself was causing to wax hotter and hotter, Richmond people were reading in the newspapers and in the *Southern Literary Messenger* the most inflammatory articles from the Northern press. Said the *New York Courier and Examiner,* of April 30, 1861 : " Let the levees on the Mississippi be at once prostrated in a hundred places while the water is high, and let the traitors and rebels living in the lower Mississippi be drowned out just as we would drown out rats infesting the hull of a ship." (It did not occur to the writer that such a procedure would be as disastrous to slaves as to masters). The *New York Tribune* of the same day suggested: " An allotment of land in Virginia will be a fitting reward for the brave fellows who have gone to fight their country's battles ", and the Philadelphia *Sunday Transcript* of May 18th advised, " Desolation from the Potomac to the Rio Grande. Let the traitor states be starved out by blockade and given to the swords and bayonets of stalwart freemen. If necessary myriads of Southern lives must be taken—Southern bodies given to the buzzards—Southern fields consigned to sterility, and Southern towns surrendered to the flames."

This stuff and more like it was read and discussed on the porches and around tea tables of " cheerful Richmond."

CHAPTER XXVIII

THE EARLIEST BATTLES

In the first field of battle of the war in Virginia, fought at Bethel Church, near Hampton, on June 10, 1861, and won by Confederates, under General Magruder, formerly of the United States Army, the Richmond Howitzers, which were first organized for the John Brown Raid, played a prominent part. Our youthful diarist, William White, was a member of the third company of this battalion. They left Chimborazo for the front " in splendid spirits ", at sunrise, on a June morning, all of the boys " eager to see service." When marching through Church Hill they passed White's home and he saw his old colored " mammy " in the yard. Let him tell it:

" She rushed into the street, clasped me in her arms and whilst great tears of grief trickled down her dusky cheek, placed in my hands a huge loaf of bread, begged me to accept it, and humbly apologized because it was all she could give. Lives the Virginian whose soul does not melt into tenderness when he remembers the ever venerated ' mammy', whose name was perhaps the first ever articulated by his childish lips, whose snow-white kerchief and kindly heart will ever be in the memories of the happy past; whose ample lap was so often childhood's couch, when tiny feet were wearied in roaming over the green fields and joyously wading through the limpid streamlets of the old homestead! And then at nightfall, when the candles were lighted, . . . how gently, tenderly, that old black ' mammy ' raised him up in her great strong arms, carried him through the spacious hall, and up the wide winding stair-case; then placing him carefully in his low trundle-bed, first taught his infant lips the hallowed words of the Lord's Prayer."

News of the victory at Bethel Church—with slight loss —was received with joy in Richmond and the work of preparation went forward with renewed zest. On July 21st, occurred that awful clash, the First Battle of Manassas. All day long the frightful carnage went on. All day long Richmond people crowded around the bulletin board—nervously, anxiously, devouring the messages from the front as fast as they could be flashed over the wires. President Davis was on the field, and at last sent word to the breathlessly waiting city:

" We have won a glorious but dear-bought victory." " Dear-bought! " It was a word South and North were to find described most victories. The shouting and the the tumult were hardly hushed when the lists of casualties began to be sent back. And now the fifes played funeral airs and muffled drums kept time as the dead came in on the trains and were borne to family sections or to the plots set apart for them in Oakwood and Hollywood. The wounded were carried to hospitals or to private homes. Blue-coated prisoners were brought in too, in great numbers, and were taken to the huge, barnlike structure, formerly a warehouse, but henceforth to be known as " Libby Prison"—and if wounded to Libby Prison Hospital. Two days after the battle of Manassas President Davis was welcomed home to Richmond by a cheering throng to whom he made a brief address praising the grey soldier boys and their commanders—General Beauregard and General Joseph E. Johnston—and lamenting the loss of General Bee, who just before his fall had rallied his men with the famous words: "There stands Jackson like a stone wall. Let us determine to die here and we will conquer."

General Winfield Scott had been regarded as a sort of son-in-law by Richmond since his marriage to one of her charming daughters, but the people could not forgive him for remaining with the United States army, which had become " the enemy." They were glad that he was in command of the defeated forces because they knew it would mean his displacement. This happened when General McClellan, known to Northerners as the "young Napoleon" of their army was given command. According to one of many stories of General Scott which have been handed down, President Lincoln asked him why, after his brilliant entrance into Mexico City, he could not get into Richmond. General Scott replied that the President must remember that many of the men who helped him to enter Mexico were the same who were keeping him out of Richmond.

On November 6th, Jefferson Davis and Alexander H. Stephens were unanimously elected as permanent President and Vice-President of the Confederacy, and Richmond chose Ex-President John Tyler to represent her in the Confederate Congress. The State Convention met again and adopted Virginia's new Constitution. The historic little white pillared building in Capitol Square was now housing the Provisional Confederate Congress, the Virginia Legislature and the Constitutional Convention at the same time. The first permanent Confederate Congress assembled in it on February 18, 1862. President Davis was inaugurated on Washington's birthday 1862, and the Square and streets leading into it were packed with people who stood in a pouring rain to see the ceremony. The President (with his Cabinet near him) stood on a platform at the base of Washington Monument with the bronze Washington immediately over his head, and the onlookers saw a good omen in the fact that the right hand of the great Revolutionary leader pointed dramatically southward. It is written that (after prayer by Bishop Johns) " Mr. Davis spoke like one inspired." That night the first of the fortnightly " levees " was held in the crowded rooms of the White House, when " The President looked weary and grave, but was all suavity and cordiality, and Mrs. Davis "—a beautiful and gracious young matron, by the way—" won all hearts by her usual unpretending kindness." These levees, were at once aristocratic and democratic. " To them " wrote one who frequented them (T. C. De Leon, in his book, *Belles, Beaux, and Brains of the Sixties*) " flocked the world and his wife, in what holiday attire they possessed, in the earlier days marked by the dainty toilettes of really elegant women, the ' butternut ' of the private soldier and the stars and yellow sashes of many a general. . .

" Mrs. Davis collected the more important of Richmond's society leaders, making of them, unawares, a sort of informal staff . . . A military band was always in attendance. . . . Cabinet ministers, congressmen, heads of bureaus and departments, new generals and old admirals fresh-faced young recruits and distinctively foreign types from the coast South, all mingled together. . . . Here was seen the red beard of Ambrose P. Hill; Beauregard would sometimes glide through the rooms with his staff. Dashing Pierce Young attended and gallants from Maryland, soft-voiced Carolinians and sturdy estrays from Kentucky and Missouri mingled with the home set and the dainty debutantes and belles. These assemblages were great amalgamators, and brought together people who had never met elsewhere." Mrs. Davis " never differentiated, and all were made to feel that they were present by right and not on sufferance. . . . The President himself unbent more at these levees—though they assuredly bored him—than anywhere else. He had that marvellous memory which locates instantly a man not seen for years and his familiar inquiries so pleased the visitors that they were not aware of being gently, but speedily, passed along."

THE EARLIEST BATTLES

The levees constituted the official entertaining of the White House. " State dinners, save in very rare necessities, as in case of important foreign visitors, were not given." Mrs. Davis was unofficially at home to visitors every evening when " only tea and talk were proffered to her guests." But, as " It was her husband's invariable custom to give one hour of each day . . . to his family circle . . . the early caller was almost sure to meet the man of the hour; to shake his courteously proffered hand; to hear the voice upon . . . which hung the fate of the Cause."

A Richmond girl (one of the lovely " three Fishers ") who attended the White House levees and was an ardent admirer of " our President ", still (as a matron of venerable age) loves to recall him. She says: " He was a stately, elegant man . . . I can see him now on his superb charger, riding through the streets unattended, and lifting his hat to all he met."

Notwithstanding the absence of so many of its men, the city overflowed with all sorts of people. In addition to members of the Confederate Congress, and the State Legislature, people having business in connection with the war were coming and going all the time. There were soldiers on leave and a swarm of refugees (whose homes had been captured or destroyed by the enemy) went from door to door seeking board and lodging in houses already crowded to the limit. Then there were more than enough pickpockets and other thieves and desperate characters of various and sundry sorts to keep Castles Thunder and Lightning filled—besides Northern spies and other undesirables. For sake of law and order President Davis proclaimed martial law in Richmond and for ten miles around it, forbade the distillation, selling, or giving away of liquor, and closed distilleries and saloons.

CHAPTER XXIX

SEVEN PINES

NEWS from Hampton Roads of the brilliant performances of the *Merrimac*—iron-covered and rechristened *Virginia*—was received in Richmond, on March 8, 1862, with wonder and admiration. Council and citizens promptly bestirred themselves to have iron-clad boats for Richmond's defense. The women decided to present the city with one of them and formed the " Ladies' Defense Association " to raise the money.

Before their plans could be carried out the Confederates saw fit to blow up the supposedly invincible *Virginia,* the enemy army was marching up the Peninsula and their gunboats were coming up the James. The gunboats received a check on May 15th, when they were driven back, badly crippled by Confederate batteries on Drewry's Bluff, eight miles below Richmond—but Richmond was in a state of alarm approaching panic. Governor Letcher called a mass-meeting that day to organize for stronger defense, and President Davis appointed the next as a day of fasting and prayer. Now all men over forty-five and boys between the ages of sixteen and eighteen were formed into a home guard, and the workers of the Tredegar Iron Works were formed into a battalion. And now all business was closed at two o'clock, that what was known as the " second class militia " might drill. By means of newspapers and bulletin boards success or failure of Southern arms in distant places was watched in Richmond with keenest joy or sorrow according to the nature of the tidings. But in Richmond itself, as Capital of the

178

Confederacy and desire of the eyes of the Federal Government and armies, interest and anxiety throughout the South centred—for all knew that if Richmond should fall the Confederacy would fall.

The gunboats knocking at one of Richmond's most important gates were being held in check, but General McClellan and his army were less than twelve miles away, overland, and were slowly, steadily coming " on to Richmond." Slowly and steadily, with march a little and dig a little, for they were throwing up earthworks as they came—making their defenses sure for deadly work—digging themselves in for a determined siege. There was but one barrier between McClellan's hosts and the coveted Capital and that was the Army of Northern Virginia under command of General Joseph E. Johnston. Within that Capital busy days were passing—busy with the rounding up of stragglers and sending them back to their places, with the movement of baggage to the rear, with the equipment of hospitals soon to be needed, busy with reinforcing the army. Richmond watched regiment after regiment of men in grey marching through town to the music of " Dixie " and " Bonny Blue Flag ", to join the lines. Many of the people and of the soldiers were impatient for something more than occasional skirmishing to happen. At last, on May 30th, all was ready for the battle expected on the morrow. A violent thunder-storm during the afternoon was followed by an unusually brilliant rainbow which seemed to exactly arch the Confederate lines. Both the soldiers and the people in the city saw in it an emblem of hope. When the sun rose next morning it saw the grey host marching along to meet the blue. Marching along, marching along, colors flying, bands playing; marching with light feet, with light hearts, gaily, gladly, as though there were no such thing in the world as screams of shot and shell, as tearing flesh and gushing blood, and faintness and pain and death. Roads were deep in mud, fields standing in water, but the men in grey were joyously marching along the Williamsburg road at last. Here and there through the tenderly green May woods gleamed spreading boughs of dogwood blossoms—like snow-white tents; here and there blushed splotches of bloom of the Judas tree—like freshly flowing wounds. But the sky was washed clean by the rain—clean of every cloud, and the morning sun glanced merrily on buttons and bayonets and on waving Confederate flags—red, white and blue like the Stars and Stripes, but different. And the men in grey were marching along, marching along to meet the men in blue.

At noon began the Battle of Seven Pines. The booming of cannon not far away filled Richmond with apprehension. Its people knew that a battle was going on— that was all. That night they knew its location and of the terrible losses to the Federals and comparatively slight losses to the Confederates. General Lee and President Davis had both been present. Just after darkness had brought surcease to the carnage and General Johnston had ordered his now weary—very, very, weary—grey soldiers to sleep on the ground where they stood, and be ready to renew the battle in the morning, he had fallen badly wounded, and had to be borne from the field. Riding into town together that night the President told General Lee that he would be, on the next day, assigned to command of the forces defending the Capital, as Johnston's wound had deprived the army " in front of Richmond " of its immediate commander and made it necessary to interfere temporarily with Lee's duties in connection with the general service. Early Sunday morning the President was again at the front, directing in person the transfer of the Army

MONUMENT AVENUE, LOOKING EAST
Lee Statue and St. James Church Spire

LEE ON "TRAVELLER" KEEPING GUARD OVER A TOBACCO FIELD ON MONUMENT AVENUE
One of Richmond's "war-gardens", summer of 1919

MONUMENT AVENUE

lor, Lewis Blair, and John Kerr Branch residences. Glimpse of Confederate Monument above the trees

of Northern Virginia to Robert E. Lee. A comparatively mild degree of fighting continued that day.

Today, in the National Cemetery at Seven Pines, monotonous row on row of small stone markers bear witness to its tragedy, and children playing in the woods nearby sometimes wonderingly pick up bullets in the grass waving above long ridges which were McClellan's breastworks.

Reports of the victory were received in Richmond with joy tempered with grief for the South's losses. Vehicles of every description were used to bring in dead and wounded and the whole town gave itself to ministering to suffering. In the barracks-like Chimborazo Hospital alone there were several thousand patients, and stores, hotels, warehouses, factories and Richmond College were turned into hospitals. Women made mattresses and churches gave their cushions for the wounded to lie upon. Great numbers of prisoners were brought in and many of them also, were sick and wounded. The blockade of Confederate ports and the seizure or destruction of food-stuffs from farms exposed to the depredations of Federal soldiers marching " on to Richmond " reduced the prisoners and patients in blue, as well as their captors, to slim rations.

CHAPTER XXX

HOSPITALS AND SOCIAL LIFE

FROM First Manassas on, nursing in homes and hospitals had been the chief employment of a large part of Richmond's population. Of course there were no professional nurses, but many girls and women were soon as proficient as if they wore graduates' badges.

Where so many performed valiant service it is possible to name but few. Mrs. Arthur F. Hopkins (née Juliet Ann Opie), of Mobile, was chosen by her State to go to Richmond and organize the Alabama Hospital, of which she became matron. She gave her fortune (of nearly $200,000) and herself to the Confederate cause. She was under fire at the battle of Seven Pines giving "first aid" to wounded men, was herself twice wounded and limped the rest of her days. General Johnston declared that she was more useful to his army than a new brigade. He was one of the line of officers, Grey and Blue, who followed her to her grave at Arlington, in 1890. The splendid work of Mrs. Lucy Mason Webb, long matron of the officer's Hospital, and that of Miss Emily Mason and her sisters are matters of record.

A commemorative tablet on a Main and Third Street house (once the residence of Judge John Robertson) marks for the passer-by of today the war-time "Sally Tompkins Hospital." Here a small, demure, young woman to become affectionately known as "Aunt Sally", worked with her many aids—women and men, white and colored —throughout the war, giving, like Mrs. Hopkins, of her means as well as her time and energy—and everybody helped her in every way. Judge John Robertson provided her with a building—his own home; hundreds of others gave money, provisions, themselves. Some gave her their family servants. Among these was Dr. Spotswood Wellford, who contributed his excellent cook. Soon after the battle of Manassas President Davis directed that only military hospitals be maintained and in order that 'little "Aunt Sally's" might be included in this class without losing its efficient head, he sent her a commission, with pay, as a Captain of Cavalry. She returned the pay to the Confederate Government, but accepted the title and "Captain Sally Tompkins" she remained for the rest of her long life.

Among the many women who nursed regularly in "Captain Sally's" hospital was Mrs. Judith McGuire, who with her husband, Rev. John P. McGuire, principal of the Episcopal High School, had been compelled to leave her home near Alexandria at the beginning of the War. She was one of the many refugees who in the city of her youth (where her father had been president of the Court of Appeals) had to walk the streets for days in search of shelter. Like many other women, she not only nursed on regular days but filled a clerical position in one of the Government Departments. Her *Diary of a Southern Refugee* (a private journal which was, later, published) gives a vivid picture of life in Richmond during the war years. Many of her patients enjoyed having the Bible read to them. She advised some of them who were depressed by the superior numbers of the Northern armies to pray, "as the Israelites did", during their wars against the Philistines. "But," replied a Georgia volunteer, "the Philistines didn't pray and the Yankees do; and though I can't bear the Yankees, I believe some of them are Christians and pray as hard as we do. I don't know what to think of our prayers clashing." Another patient hearing of one of the frequent days of fasting and prayer appointed by President Davis asked: "I wonder if Mars' Jeff himself fasts on these days?" And was informed that he did, and attended the services too.

Ministers and Young Men's Christian Association men did splendid work for the soldiers—in hospitals and out of them. In January, 1863, Rev. Moses D. Hoge, D. D. was sent to England to solicit Bibles for them. He brought back 10,000 copies of the Bible, 50,000 of the New Testament and 25,000 of the Gospels and Psalms.

Hard as times were many home-made delicacies—thin biscuits, broths, jellies and so on—which the people could not think of indulging in themselves, found their way to the bedsides of sick and wounded soldiers. Even the children did their bit toward making the patients comfortable—fanning flies away from feverish faces with paper fans made in the spare moments of Richmond women.

Hear Mrs. McGuire tell a story illustrating the attitude toward the war of the plain people who never had owned and never expected to own a slave, and surely would not have given their lives and their all rather than have the "upper ten" lose the right to own them.

Seeing a woman of this class buying Confederate grey cloth at a fancy price in a store, Mrs. McGuire told her that she could get it much cheaper from the quartermaster. She replied:

"I know all about that, for my three sons is in the army, and gets their clothes *thar;* but you see this is for my old man, and I don't think it would be fair to get his clothes from *thar,* because he ain't never done nothing for the country *as yet.* He's just *gwine* in the army . . . He says to me, says he, ' The country wants me; I wonder if I could stand marching?' . . . . Says I, ' Old man, I don't think you could, you would break down; but . . .

184

FRANKLIN STREET OPPOSITE MONROE PARK

The ante-bellum State Fair Grounds. On the left, Davenport, Peter and Scott residences and Pace Memoria

WEST FRANKLIN STREET

Showing Hotel Jefferson, the Archer Anderson residence, and the Second Baptist Church

you can drive a wagon in the place of a young man that's driving, and the young man can fight.' . . . And he's agwine just as soon as I gits these clothes ready." "Did you want your sons to go?" "Want 'em to go? Yes; if they hadn't agone, they shouldn't a-staid whar I was. But they wanted to go, *my* sons did!" She added: "Them Yankees must not come a-nigh to Richmond; if they does, I will fight them myself. The women must fight, for they shan't cross Mayo's Bridge; they shan't git to Richmond!"

Many of the older men, besides being members of the home-guard and ambulance corps worked in the hospitals. From first to last 1,300 men nursed in the Sally Tompkins hospital.

All life was strange, very, very strange in Richmond in those days. At St. Paul's Church, on a February Sunday morning in 1862 the sermon was preached by Rev. Mr. Quintard, then a Chaplain in the army, who was Bishop Quintard of a later period. He wore his surplice over his Chaplain's uniform. Says Mrs. McGuire: "It was strange to see the bright military buttons gleam beneath the canonicals. Everything is strange now!"

But all was not sadness and gloom, even in those times that tried men's souls. General Lee urged the pretty girls who flocked around him eager for a smile or a hand-clasp, to make their homes as gay as possible for the soldiers on leave in Richmond. "Which" (in the words of one of "the three Fishers") "we always tried to do. . . .

"It was understood that young ladies were ready to receive in the afternoon and evening, and the soldier boys would call in great numbers. Frequently the girls would meet at one particular home. We would have music and dancing—cotillions and quadrilles, ending with the old Virginia reel. . . . Sometimes there would be one belle, who appeared in handsome velvet or satin, trimmed with point lace, that had been worn by an ancestress, while others in the room would feel very elegant in a wash muslin or a calico dress, costing, perhaps, fifteen dollars a yard (in Confederate money). On one occasion I wore an old tarleton dress, resurrected, rumpled and worn, from the depths of an antique trunk. I had no trimming for it, except rows of arbor vitæ, which I plucked from a tree in the yard. . . . As the war went on we had little but homespun dresses . . . which we wore with great pride over big hoop skirts. . . . I remember a hat that I made out of an old broadcloth coat and it had a feather on it that came from the waving plume of a chanticleer."

An answer to the question why was pain permitted to come into the world may never be found. Perhaps one reason was to give the human heart a chance to show its power to rebound. Happily, wartime youth is the same perennial as peacetime youth—under different circumstances; and even war cannot make prigs and prudes of wholesome-minded young folk. As the war went on " starvation parties" were popular. Richmond boys and girls could make feasts of lemonade very nearly minus lemons and sugar, served with cakes minus almost any of the conventional ingredients. Richmond girls could be bewitching in straw hats plaited by their own fingers of blades of rye and in party frocks fashioned out of old lace curtains or any old furbelows found in attics. A girl who secured enough black alpaca to make herself a dress in the voluminous style of the time and enough bright colored skirt braid to trace upon it a " wall of Troy " design, with knots of the braid instead of ribbon at her throat and upon her hair, was admired by all of her chums.

Not only for party finery were attics ransacked, but for materials of which to contrive costumes and stage

DRAWING-ROOMS OF THE WESTMORELAND CLUB

Originally the Stanard House, built by the husband of Poe's "Helen," and in which, during the occupancy
was a guest

By courtesy of Mr. Robert A. Lancaster, Jr.

properties for amateur theatricals and tableaux which served the double purpose of providing diversion and making money for charity. There were always women and girls enough for the feminine parts and any man—from a private to a general—who happened to be spending a night in Richmond, was in danger of being pressed into service for a masculine rôle. General "Jeb" Stuart was once captured for a star part in a tableau and appeared in full uniform. The McGuire Diary pauses in its record of anguish in 1863 to tell of the disappointment of Richmond girls because a brigade which had planned to give a tournament was ordered away. For the quiet and cultured set there were innumerable musicales and the unique literary and musical entertainments of the "Mosaic Club." There were also dinners and receptions for military heroes and others in many private homes. De Leon names as among especially hosttesses Mrs. Samuels, Mrs. Macfarland, Mrs. Ives and Mrs. Pegram. He adds: "What came nearest to a *Salon* in Richmond—and as far as I know in America— was held at Mrs. Robert C. Stanard's. . . . At her frequent dinners, receptions and evenings, Mrs. Stanard collected most that was brilliant and brainiest in government, army and congress. . . . There, men met statesmen like Lamar, Benjamin, Soulé and their peers; jurists like John A. Campbell and Thomas J. Semmes; fighters like Johnson, Hampton and Gordon; and the most polished and promising youth of the war. . . . And with these came the best of her own sex that the tact and experience of the hostess could select. . . . Her house was one unremittent *Salon*." This Mrs. Stanard was the same who had been Thackeray's hostess in the house which has been the home of the Westmoreland Club for more than a generation— the same whose husband had been Poe's playmate.

CHAPTER XXXI

THE SEVEN DAYS' BATTLES AROUND RICHMOND

AFTER " Seven Pines ", the Grey army was more than ever determined to die rather than let the enemy at the gates of the Capital come in. People and soldiers were heartened by news of Stonewall Jackson's brilliant performance in the Valley of Virginia. He was keeping General McDowell too busy there for him to be sent to carry out the enemy's plan of reinforcing McClellan in his siege of Richmond. Lee knew that McClellan was strongly intrenched in front of him and on his left, and planned to attack his right wing so soon as he could be certain of its location. The intrepid cavalry leader, General J. E. B. Stuart, with 1,200 cavalry and a battery of artillery, undertook to get him this information. To use General Lee's own words, General Stuart with " part of the troops under his command . . . made a reconnoissance between the Pamunkey and Chickahominy Rivers and succeeded in passing around the rear of the whole Union Army, routing the enemy in a series of skirmishes, taking a number of prisoners, destroying and capturing stores to a large amount. Having most successfully accomplished its object, the expedition recrossed the Chickahominy almost in the presence of the enemy, with the same coolness and address that marked every step of the progress and with the loss of but one man, the lamented Captain Latané, of the Ninth Virginia Cavalry, who fell leading a successful charge against a force of the enemy." With the information thus acquired in his hands, General Lee planned his next step. Jackson suddenly disappeared from the Valley—causing all sorts of wild guesses—but General Lee knew that he was quietly moving his forces southward, toward Richmond. On June 23d, he left his army at Fredericks Hall and rode on alone. That night he was in secret conference with Lee, Longstreet and the two Hills, " somewhere " near Richmond. On June 26th, Jackson's Army moved from Ashland, about fifteen miles north of Richmond, eastward toward Mechanicsville, to join General A. P. Hill. He had arrived in Ashland half a day later than was planned and General Hill had already crossed the Chickahominy at Meadow Bridge and moved on the tiny village of Mechanicsville, driving Federal forces before him.

These actors in a great tragedy were all unconscious of the audience watching them from a gallery furnished by the hills and roofs of Richmond. Let Mrs. McGuire tell it : " Early in the morning it was whispered about that some great movement was on foot. Large numbers of troops were seen under arms. . . . A. P. Hill's division occupied the range of hills near ' Strawberry Hill ' the cherished [summer] home of my childhood. About three o'clock in the morning the order to move . . . was given. . . . The gallant Fortieth followed by Pegram's Battery rushed across the bridge at double quick and with exultant shouts drove the enemy's pickets from their posts. The enemy was driven rapidly down the river to Mechanicsville [3½ miles east of Meadow Bridge and 8 miles north of Richmond] where the battle raged long and fiercely. At nine o'clock all was quiet. . . . Our victory is said to be glorious but not complete. . . . Our streets were thronged until a late hour to catch the last accounts from couriers and spectators. . . . The President and many others were on the surrounding hills during the fight, deeply interested spectators. The calmness of the people during the progress of the battle was marvellous. The balloons of the

189

enemy hovering over the battle field could be distinctly seen from the outskirts of the city, and the sound of musketry as distinctly heard, but none were alarmed for the safety of the city. From the firing of the first gun till the close of the battle every spot favorable for observation was crowded. The tops of the Exchange and the Ballard House, the Capitol, and almost every other tall house were covered with human beings, and after nightfall the commanding hills from the President's house to the Alms House were covered like a vast amphitheatre with men, women and children witnessing the grand display of fireworks—beautiful, yet awful, and sending death amid those our hearts hold so dear. . . . The brilliant lights of bombs bursting in the air and the passing to the ground of innumerable lesser lights, emitted by the thousands and thousands of muskets with the roar of artillery and the rattling of small arms constituted a scene terrifically grand."

Finally, both Blue and Grey soldiers slept on their arms, awaiting daylight and renewal of the battle. The great war-stage north of Richmond had become a giant chess-board whose players moved their men back and forth in their effort to accomplish a checkmate. At dawn next day the battle was renewed, but during the night McClellan had retired from his strongly fortified position along Beaver Dam Creek to one greatly strengthened by breast works and abatis along Powhite Creek (another branch of the Chickahominy, five miles further east) and there the battles of Gaines' Mill and Cold Harbor were fought next day. At ten o'clock that night Mrs. McGuire jotted down in her Diary: "Another day of great excitement in our beleaguered city. From early dawn the cannon have been roaring around us. Our success has been glorious! The citizens—gentlemen as well as ladies—

have been fully occupied in the hospitals. Kent, Paine &
Co. have thrown open their spacious building for the use
of the wounded. . . . General Jackson has joined General
Lee and nearly the whole army on both sides were engaged.
The enemy has retired before our troops to their strong
works near Gaines' Mill. Brigade after brigade of our
brave men were hurled against them, and repulsed in
disorder. McClellan is said to be retreating. Praise the
Lord, O my soul!"

On June 29th, the Grey force met with continued success at Savage Station; on the next day at Frazier's Farm.
On July 1st, Jackson in his pursuit, found McClellan
splendidly fortified at historic "Malvern Hill", the old
Cocke home, on a high bluff overlooking James River, a
few miles below Richmond. "The battle raged until
late into the night, but all efforts to pierce the enemy's
line failed—" wrote General Lee's adjutant, Col. Walter
H. Taylor. During the night McClellan's army folded
their tents and stole away. It is written that they left
"their dead unburied and their wounded as they fell,"
and that "the wheatfields about 'Shirley' [the ancestral
home of General Lee's mother] were all trampled down
by the fugitives too impatient to follow the road. Arms,
accoutrements, knapsacks and overcoats were strewn on
the roadside and in the field." The McGuire Diary
brings its record of the Seven Days' Battles to a close
with: "Richmond is disenthralled and the only Yankees
there are in the Libby and other prisons. McClellan and
his 'Grand Army' are on James River near 'Westover',
enjoying mosquitoes and bilious fevers." General Lee's
report says in part: "The siege of Richmond was
raised. The object of the campaign which had been
prosecuted after months of preparation, at an enormous
expenditure of men and money, completely frustrated."

Prior to this time, General Lee had been intensely admired in Richmond and the South; after it he was adored.

During the Seven Days' Battles, Richmond had its hands full caring for the wounded, burying the dead and providing for the prisoners. Hospitals and homes were overflowing. Libby Prison was so packed that many prisoners were taken to Belle Isle, opposite Gamble's Hill. Exchange of prisoners going on all the time brought relief to both Blue and Grey. The Blue soldiers did not spend July 4th in Richmond, as victors, as they had planned, but about that time Richmond gazed silently on three thousand of them who had been prisoners of war, being marched out of town. They were a homesick, heartsick, hungry lot, and were happy to shake the city's red clay dust from their feet, for they had seen little of its hospitality in those days of blockade, siege and detestation of blue uniforms.

About two miles from the point where fell Captain William Latané—the only man lost by General Stuart in his passage around McClellan's army—were the adjoining Brockenbrough and Newton plantations, "Westwood" and "Summer Hill." Captain Latané's brother, giving his horse to a soldier whose own mount had been shot under him, remained beside the body, while his comrades swept on. Seeing the "Westwood" mill-cart on its way to the mill with sacks of corn to be ground, he hailed it. "Uncle Aaron," the old negro driver helped him to lift his dead brother into it and drove it back to "Westwood", whose mistress Mrs. Catherine Brockenbrough, the only white person on the place, received it tenderly, promised to give it burial, and sped the brother on his way on a horse which the "Summer Hill" family had managed to hide from the enemy.

Mrs. Brockenbrough, with the help of her niece, Mrs.

"THE BURIAL OF LATANÉ"
From a steel engraving of the wartime painting by William D. Washington

"CAPTAIN" SALLY TOMPKINS, CONFEDERATE WAR NURSE

William B. Newton, mistress of " Summer Hill " and her sister-in-law, Mrs. Willoughby Newton, who was refugeeing there, prepared the body for burial and had a pine coffin made for it at " Westwood " Carpenter Shop. " Uncle Aaron " dug the grave in " Summer Hill " graveyard and was sent to ask Rev. Mr. Caraway to read the funeral service; but the blue-coat pickets would not permit the aged minister to pass, and so, next day, the ladies of the two households (which included the Misses Dabney, refugeeing at " Summer Hill ") with the aid of some of the family servants, buried him themselves. Mrs. Willoughby Newton read the service from the Prayer Book and Mrs. William Newton's little children (whose father was soon to be killed leading a cavalry charge) strewed flowers on the grave. John R. Thompson wrote a poem, which was published in the *Southern Literary Messenger,* describing the incident. William D. Washington read the poem and made the scene the subject of a much admired painting, which has been lost, but has become noted through reproduction. Many copies of a steel engraving made from it may be seen in Richmond and other Southern homes today. Wartime Richmond belles posed for the figures. Mrs. Newton reading the burial service is represented by the beautiful Page Waller (later Mrs. Legh Page), and the other figures in the picture are Mattie Waller (Mrs. Ralph C. Johnson, of Washington), Lizzie Giles (Mrs. Samuel Robinson, of Washington), Jennie Pegram (Mrs. David McIntosh of Baltimore), Mattie Paul (Mrs. William Myers, of Richmond) and Imogen Warwick and Annie Gibson, representing the little Newton girls—Lucy and Kate.

The youthful General Stuart was made forever famous by his ride around McClellan. His flowing chestnut beard, floating white plume and the merry twinkle in his eye were as familiar a part of him as his snugly fitting grey cloth and his gilt stars, buttons and spurs. He was as chivalrous in the drawing-room as he was dashing and fearless on the field, and to the girls, seemed as romantic a figure as any knight of old. He had his serious side— was a devoted Christian and never drank nor swore—but at the same time bubbled with fun and humor and had a boyish zest for a good time. When it was not necessary for him to fight, fight, fight, what he loved best was to dance, dance, dance, with the lightest footed girl he could fling his arm around to the music of a popular waltz. Soon after his dash around McClellan he was at a ball in Richmond at which pretty Lizzie Giles wore a " really and truly " party frock, made of tulle which had run the blockade. Of course General Stuart must whirl that fairy-like figure about whom floated yards upon yards of snowy thistle-down, around the ballroom floor. He danced in spurs and one of them caught in the airy stuff swirling after the dancer's twinkling slippers, tearing off streamers of it which wound themselves around and around the young general's cavalry boots; but in a trance of joy, he would not stop, nor let his partner stop. So they kept whirling, whirling, whirling until much of the tulle was in tatters. Scarce as tulle party frocks were, the fair wearer, if she could speak today, would say: " It was worth it ! "

Magazine and newspaper jokes reflect the spirit of the time in Richmond in those years when the Confederacy was still full of hope. The *Messenger* for January, 1862, has a burlesque on an examination of a Federal soldier for a commission. " ' Are you familiar with the history of General Scott? ' the applicant is supposed to be asked. ' You can bet on it ' is the reply. ' General Scott was born in Virginia at an early age. He licked the British in 1812, wrote the Waverly Novels and his son Whahae bled with

THE CATHEDRAL OF THE SACRED HEART, FROM MONROE PARK

SYNAGOGUE OF THE CONGREGATION OF BETH AHABAH
By courtesy of Rabbi Edward N. Calisch, Ph.D.

Wallace.' 'Pause, fair youth. What makes you think that General Scott had a son named Whahae?' 'Ha!... that's because you don't understand poickry. Why if you will just turn to Burns' works, you will learn that Scott's Wha'hae wi' Wallace bled.'

"The Board was so pleased with Villiam's learning that it gave him his commission, presenting him with two gunboats and a cannon, and recommended him for President of the New York Historical Society."

Stuart, on his raid around McClellan's Army, is described by the *Richmond Examiner* as "a circuit rider conducting a series of missionary meetings" and reporting his success to "Bishop" Robert E. Lee. "Even their wagons were converted and purified by fire. Some of them were constrained to come and abide with us, bringing with them their cattle."

A writer in the Richmond *Whig* jocularly describes Jackson as a man dangerous to the peace of society and issues a mock proclamation signed "Jefferson Davison," offering $1,000 reward "if the aforesaid Stonewall is taken in Washington, $5,000 if taken in Philadelphia, and $20,000 if taken in Portland, Maine."

There never was a human being more ready for a bit of laugh-provoking nonsense than a tired, ragged, dirty, hungry Confederate soldier.

CHAPTER XXXII

ON TO RICHMOND AGAIN

On December 14, 1862, cannonading in the direction of Fredericksburg, heard in Ashland, announced that a new " on to Richmond " expedition under McClellan's successor, General Burnside, was being vigorously repulsed. Mrs. McGuire (who was then in Ashland) wrote: " The firing is very heavy and incessant. We hear it with terrible distinctness from our portico. God of Mercy be with our people and keep back the invaders! I ask not their destruction; but that they be driven to their homes, nevermore to set foot on our soil." The next day she wrote: " Trains have been constantly passing with the wounded for the Richmond hospitals. . . . Ladies were at every depot with refreshments." *History repeats itself.*

Though frequent skirmishing kept the people uneasy and the news of battles far away and the coming in of the wounded and prisoners were depressing signs of the times, Richmond was not the centre of hostilities again for some time following the battle of Fredericksburg. But conditions in the city grew more and more distressing. Confederate money had become almost worthless and the problem of finding food to keep together souls and bodies of dwellers in homes, hospitals and prisons more and more difficult. On April 2, 1863, a mob of rough boys and women, armed with knives and hatchets entered the Confederate Commissary and helped themselves from its meagre stores. The Mayor, the Governor and the President each in turn remonstrated with them, but not until the Home Guard was called out and ordered to fire, was the " Bread Riot " quelled.

196

ON TO RICHMOND AGAIN

After Burnside's failure at Fredericksburg General Hooker was put in his place and another " on to Richmond " march was made ; but he, too, found checkmate—this time, on May 31st, at Chancellorsville. But the victory was the costliest yet, for Stonewall Jackson whom the South was beginning to regard as invincible—immortal, almost—was severely wounded and in Richmond the peace of taps-hour, on a fragrant May Sunday was broken by by the news of his death. Jackson dead? Jackson dead? The people repeated the question over and over again staring at one another with pallid faces. On the next afternoon, while all of the church bells which had not been melted to make cannon were tolling, the train bringing his coffin wrapped in a Confederate flag and covered with flowers placed upon it by Ashland people when it passed through, came into stricken Richmond and stopped at Broad and Sixth Streets. It was removed to a hearse and, while the band played a dirge, escorted by military and people to the Governor's house. Next day it lay in state in the Capitol where the great soldier's noble and beloved face was viewed by heart-broken thousands. On Wednesday they took him home to Lexington.

Jackson dead? Yes, yet forever living, not only in the Beyond, but here—in History, and in the heart of each succeeding generation of Southerners. Today in Richmond, a sculptured figure stands on a pedestal in Capitol Square facing the white pillared house of many happenings. It was placed there long ago by English admirers of him it represents. Children tell one another it is Stonewall Jackson and grow up familiar with the look of him and with stories of his heroic deeds. And away toward the sunset in the middle of the finest street of the Richmond which has arisen on the ruins of the Confederacy's Capital, passersby may see him, in memorial bronze, on his favorite horse, " Sorrel." Rider and horse in perfect repose, looking serenely Northward—day after day, year in year out, he stands there like a stonewall.

Richmond and the whole South fully realized the loss of General Jackson when the news came of the disastrous battle at Gettysburg on the first day of July, 1863, between the Grey army under General Lee and the Blue under General Meade—who had succeeded Hooker. Orders for Libby Prison to make ready for 6,000 prisoners were followed by the dreaded dead and missing list. The sorrowing people told one another as they read it that if General Lee had only had the aid of Stonewall Jackson he would have won another great victory.

The third year of the war dragged on in Richmond with war work given over more and more to women, as the need of men at the front became greater. There was of course endless knitting, lint-scraping and sewing, in addition to nursing, and many women filled places in the government departments. Meanwhile, news from the battlefields north, south and in Virginia, was breathlessly watched for and anxiously discussed. With the spring had come relief from the high tension under which soldiers and people were living, in the form of a wartime " best seller." Notwithstanding the difficulty of carrying on any kind of business, " West and Johnston " had managed to bring out a number of eagerly read books—among them reprints of some of the novels of Wilkie Collins and a translation of Octave Fuillet's *Romance of a Poor Young Man*. *The Messenger* for February, 1863, announced a translation of *Les Misérables*, in five parts, at $2.00 a part. Copies of the first part— " Fantine "—in flimsy pamphlet form, were bought, passed along and read to tatters. A soldier who had seen it advertised went into a Richmond store and asked for " Lee's

Miserables faintin'. " The story went the rounds and throughout the South " Lee's Miserables " became the jocular name for Victor Hugo's masterpiece. The July *Messenger* announced that " Fantine " was in its tenth thousand and that the second part of the book—" Cosette " —would be ready soon. The July *Messenger* also devoted thirteen closely printed pages to a review of " Fantine." The August number contained a fifteen page notice of " Cosette " and announced that the three other parts would be issued in one volume as soon as paper could be secured.

The year 1864 opened with a little ripple of social life. President and Mrs. Davis held a New Year's Day reception in honor of the inauguration of a new Governor of Virginia—" Extra Billy " Smith—and on January 9th, the people gave a ball at the Ballard House in honor of Gen. John B. Morgan, who had escaped from an Ohio prison and made his way to Richmond.

On February 28th, the Bell in the Tower warned the city of the approach, by way of Brook Road, of General Kilpatrick with a column of cavalry detached from Meade's army—then near Orange, Virginia. All business stopped and every man who could bear arms marched out under General Wilcox, to the city's defense. Meantime, General Lee (who was in the neighborhood of Orange, hourly expecting a clash with Meade), was informed by wire of the impending raid and sent a detachment under General Wade Hampton to the rescue, with disastrous results to the enemy. A day or two later a second column of Kilpatrick's command, under Colonel Dahlgren, attempted a more daring raid. With himself and men clad in Confederate uniforms, he came within three miles of Richmond, but was repulsed with loss of forty of his four hundred men. Some of the remaining forces went off to join Kilpatrick while the rest escaped with Dahlgren and entered King and Queen County. There, a home guard of old men of the county lay in wait for them in the woods, at a spot which has ever since been known as " Dahlgren's Corner ", and suddenly opened fire. Dahlgren fell dead, a number of his men were killed and ninety white men and thirty-five negroes were captured. His plans, disclosed by written orders found on his person, were: " Release the prisoners from Belle Isle first and having seen them fairly started we will cross James River into Richmond, destroying the bridges after us, and exhorting the released prisoners to destroy and burn the hateful city, and do not allow the rebel leader, Davis, to escape . . . . Be prepared with oakum, turpentine and torpedoes. Destroy everything that can be used by the rebels. Shoot horses, cattle, destroy the railroads and the canal, burn the city, leave only the hospitals and kill Jeff Davis and his Cabinet." Dahlgren's body was sent to Richmond, and was buried by Confederate soldiers in Oakwood Cemetery. His father, Admiral Dahlgren, sent President Davis a hundred dollars in gold, with the request that his son's body be sent home, but the grave was empty. Miss Van Lew—the Federal spy—and some of her friends, had had the body taken up, placed in a metallic coffin and buried beyond the city. After the War it was again disinterred and sent to Admiral Dahlgren. General Meade emphatically disclaimed knowledge or approval of Dahlgren's orders.

In May, 1864, the whole Confederacy was thrilled by the gallantry of the Virginia Military Institute cadets at the Battle of New Market. Some of these young heroes were Richmond boys and years afterward their valor was commemorated with an impressive monument by another son of Virginia's capital, the famous sculptor, Sir Moses Ezekiel.

CHAPTER XXXIII

ENTER GENERAL GRANT

ULYSSES S. GRANT (supplanting Meade) was the next general chosen to lead the Federal Army "on to Richmond." He opened his campaign May 4, 1864, by moving the great army raised for him across the Rapidan River and southward, but was checkmated with frightful loss, by General Lee, in the battles of the Wilderness and Spotsylvania Court House. His dispatch to Washington, of May 10th, said: "The enemy . . . evince a very strong purpose to interpose between us to the last." But General Grant was determined to bring to pass the fall of Richmond and the Confederacy if there should be no one left on either side to tell the tale. It is written in his official report: "The resources of the enemy and his numerical strength were far inferior to ours." With this knowledge of superior strength to make him certain of ultimate success, he called for and received reinforcement after reinforcement, with abundant fresh supplies of ammunition and rations. To consider the value of human life was to fail, and he was determined not to fail! He hurled his reinforcements upon the thinning ranks of Lee's men who gallantly rushed forward to meet them, with their "rebel yell"—weird and triumphant as the cry of the Valkyries—and (in the words of Col. Walter H. Taylor) "their earnest faces, their sparkling eyes, their cheeks, in many cases begrimed, their tattered clothing, their bright rifles."

During the terrific carnage which went on for days at Spotsylvania (afterward fitly named "the Bloody Angle") Grant sent Sheridan with 10,000 cavalry around Lee's right wing toward Richmond. Stuart, learning of the plan, followed with three brigades, two of which were to hedge Sheridan off before he could reach Richmond and the third to attack him from the rear. Stuart, with his 3,000 reached Yellow Tavern (on Brook Road, six miles north of Richmond) on May 11th, and held Sheridan's 10,000 men in check nearly all day (until Bragg had time to bring his troops from below Richmond to relieve him) after which Sheridan retreated back to Grant's Army. Thus, a second time, "Jeb" Stuart saved Richmond—but while leading the charge he received a mortal wound and died there next day. To President Davis who visited him a few hours before the end, this gay-hearted young warrior, known as the "eyes and ears of Lee's army", said: "I am willing to die if God and my country think I have fulfilled my destiny and done my duty."

Again Richmond hospitals and prisons were overflowing, and with the purchasing power of Confederate money so low that flour was selling at $400 a barrel and other supplies at proportionate prices. General Grant with his large, well-equipped army was pushing "on to Richmond"—the now sorely harassed Richmond—from the northward, and General Butler, with his, from the southward. By the time June's first roses were blowing in the gardens and birds in the trees overhanging the river were—all unmindful of the horrors of war—singing to The Falls of the joys of summertime, Lee's army was strongly entrenched before Richmond. His inner line of breastworks to the westward are now covered by stately Monument Avenue, where, in bronze to which time is giving the greenish gray mold poetically suggestive of the tint of Confederate uniforms, sits Lee on faithful "Traveller."

ENTER GENERAL GRANT

Facing the Grey army to the northward Grant's 120,000 men formed a glittering double and triple battle line over ground where Confederate forces had been victorious in the Seven Days' Battles two years before. And they were to be victorious again. On the afternoon of June 3d, Richmond people heard constant cannon-thunder for one hour during which twelve thousand of the boys in Blue who heroically obeyed the order that hurled them against the Grey wall standing between them and the city of their desire, joined the ranks of the dead and missing. "Theirs not to reason why." For the space of one hour two hundred men a minute killed or wounded for the sake of getting into Richmond! In the space of one hour the Second Battle of Cold Harbor had passed into history and notwithstanding the sacrifice of twelve thousand men Richmond was safe—as yet—as yet. Even the small percentage of Lee's thinning army which gallantly fell to keep Richmond safe a little longer was serious enough to the Confederates.

While the Blue and Grey armies still faced each other the officers and men of the 26th Mississippi Regiment offered to divide their slim rations for the next two days with the starving women and children of besieged Richmond. Mayor Mayo thankfully accepted the offer.

General Grant now requested a truce that he might bury the dead piled up before his lines, and care for his wounded. Then, after moving his forces off toward the east he gave up hope of capturing Richmond for a time, and crossed the river to lay siege to Petersburg. But the Grey wall whose look had become familiar stood between him and that city also—for Lee was there before him. The tug of war before Petersburg continued day after day, week after week, month after month. July 30th the Battle of the Crater was fought, with Federal loss of 4,000 to

Confederate of only 800; but the Blue reinforcements seemed limitless while the Grey lines were gradually and permanently thinning—thinning—thinning. During the Petersburg siege futile, but alarming, raids on Richmond continued. Over and over again the Bell in the Tower closed up business and sent every man who could bear arms to the defense of the city. Under fire of Confederate batteries atop the bluff a few miles down the river, Ben Butler was making Confederate prisoners dig a canal across Dutch Gap to provide a short passage " on to Richmond ", for Federal gunboats—an enterprise for the purpose of destroying the city which was to fail, but which when (after the war) it was completed by United States Government Engineers, became, and still is, of great commercial benefit to Richmond and its neighborhood.

News came to Richmond of disasters in the South; in Maryland; of General Early's defeat in the Valley of Virginia; of Sherman's ghastly march through Georgia. There were some successes still, but many discouragements. The people grew despondent. Winter came on, bringing Christmas—the darkest Christmas in Richmond's history. " Peace on Earth, good will to men," seemed meaningless phrases. Yet people strove to be cheerful. Confederate money bought less than ever. Turkeys were from fifty to a hundred dollars apiece, but every home that could manage it had something in the way of a little feast— if only ginger cakes made with sorghum. The new year opened with besieged Petersburg still keeping the armies of Lee and Grant busy, while the people there and in Richmond waited and suffered, and depression deepened —deepened—deepened. Slowly, anxiously, miserably, January passed. Carpets which had covered big old-fashioned rooms, were cut up into squares, whipped around the edges to keep them from ravelling and used for bed coverings in the hospitals and in tents. Old men were sent around to gather up lead tops of preserving jars to be melted into bullets. Women gave their silver, their jewelry—anything that could be sold—to buy food for the soldiers. Men gave their watches. February came and went. In the midst of its anguish Richmond rejoiced that General Lee was made Commander-in-Chief of all the Southern armies. Early in March, through a letter to General Grant, he made an attempt to treat for peace, but President Lincoln refused a conference for that purpose.

CHAPTER XXXIV

THE FALL OF RICHMOND

WAITING Richmond knew that with ports open and
means to buy supplies and to hire troops from outside
of the country, as well as power to draft those inside,
the blue coats had the world to draw on, for both men
and materials; and hope of saving the city grew dimmer
and dimmer. Spring's pale green veil rested on grove
and garden. Jonquils and hyacinths were blooming again;
birds singing again. All nature was prating of hope and
renewal of life. But on Friday, the last day of March,
Mrs. McGuire scribbled in her Diary: " Many persons
think that Richmond . . . may be evacuated at any time."
On the next day booming of cannon from the Southward told of the Battle of " Five Forks " going on before
Petersburg. The mournful sounds sent shivers of apprehension through Richmond, for the weakness of the vanishing Grey army was realized there. The next day was
Sunday—a beautiful April Sunday. Half way up the
middle aisle of St. Paul's sat the President of the Confederacy, listening to the Rector's sermon. A messenger
entered the church, walked up the aisle, stopped and
whispered to Mr. Davis, who took up his hat and went
quickly out. Richmond soon knew what it meant. The
battered Grey wall before Petersburg had given way.
The town had fallen. General Lee had ordered General
Ewell in command of forces in and about Richmond to
evacuate the city—to move all troops, artillery, infantry,
cavalry and all military wagons, burning the bridges behind them. Cotton and tobacco were to be destroyed to
prevent their capture.

THE FALL OF RICHMOND

Consternation was followed by despair. People who could get themselves and their goods out of the doomed city did not wait for the military to leave. The bars were down and "the enemy" which had for four years clamored for entrance would soon rush in. President Davis and other officials made arrangements to be off before they were captured. "In the shortest time imaginable vehicles of all kinds were flying along bearing goods of all sorts and people of all ages and classes." At midnight committees named by the City Council began their work of pouring into the gutters all the liquor in town, and before daybreak the torch was applied to cotton and tobacco in the warehouses. The soft spring night was still, and it was believed that the fires could be controlled, but as dawn approached a wind sprang up blowing from the wholesale district toward the heart of the business section. The flames leaped and crackled, licking hungrily at—devouring—building after building, and went laughing and shouting on their ruinous way. Among homes threatened was that of General Lee, on which streams of water played all day. A lawless mob rushed ahead of the flames and carried away everything they could snatch —in carts, in wheelbarrows and in their arms.

Soon after sunrise a brigade of Grey cavalry rode into the city with expectation of taking part in its defense. A white flag on a parapet by the roadside and the " dense smoke which seemed to be rising from every direction " told them of the fall of the Confederacy's Capital. " As our column moved slowly through the mob, using sabres to clear the way ", wrote Private Spottswood Bird, of this brigade, " this mass of every age, sex and color, wild with excitement, and many laden with plunder, would block our way at every turn. The streets and sidewalks were filled with boxes, barrels, timbers and goods of every kind and description. As barrels, boxes, etc., were rolled from the stores, the mob would burst them open and scramble wildly for the contents, apparently regardless of whether they became victims of the flames, were trampled beneath our horses' feet, or fell under the blows of our sabres, in their wild greed for loot. In one of the warehouses they found a quantity of whisky stored, and as the barrels were rolled into the street they were met by those outside, promptly burst open with clubs, the contents literally filling the gutters as from a shower of rain. Numbers of them grabbed up tubs and buckets, dipped to the brim the fiery liquid, which the more generous of them freely dispensed to our men with the tin cans, cups, etc., lying around. This served as the only breakfast we had; it was better than none, and in keeping with the surroundings."

Immediately after the Confederate troops were gone Mayor Mayo with a special Committee carrying a flag of truce rode out to the fortifications beyond Tree Hill farm to surrender the Southern Capital. He delivered this letter:

Richmond, Monday, April 3, 1865.
To the General Commanding the United States Army in front of Richmond.
General:—The Army of the Confederate Government having abandoned the City of Richmond, I respectfully request that you will take possession of it with an organized force, to preserve order and protect women and children and property.
Respectfully,
Joseph Mayo, Mayor.

When the fire was at its height a cry of wild distress swept through town: " The Yankees! The Yankees have taken our city! "

General Weitzel at the head of triumphantly hurrahing Blue cavalry dashed through the streets. The big iron gates of Capitol Square swung wide to receive them and

THE EVACUATION AND BURNING OF RICHMOND, APRIL 2, 1865
Old Mayo's Bridge in the foreground
From a contemporary engraving

RING RICHMOND, IMMEDIATELY AFTER ITS EVACUATION, APRIL 3, 1865. VIEW FROM MAIN
AND NINTH STREETS, LOOKING EAST

From a contemporary engraving. By courtesy of First National Bank

over the greensward they rode to the white-pillared Capitol. Some of them were hardly dismounted before they were flying up the steps. Past the halls of many conventions, past the Houdon Washington, they sped, to the top of the building. The Stars and Bars were hauled down; the Stars and Stripes flung to the breeze. The four years' dream of " On to Richmond " had come true at last!

But it was a distressed and distracted Richmond which was entered. The military was for the most part courteous and the people gladly coöperated with them in their efforts to restore order. They succeeded in getting the fire under control by blowing up buildings in its path, but not until nine hundred houses (mills, factories, stores, dwellings and their contents) and four-fifths of the whole supply of food in the city—and also a church—had been destroyed. Half a mile of Main Street, with portions of intersecting streets, were smoking debris in the midst of which rose blackened walls with shutterless windows, like ghastly eyes staring upon the scene of desolation, and here and there a lonely chimney.

Martial law was declared. General Shepley, Military Governor of the city, made the Capitol his headquarters. General Devers was given the Governor's Mansion and Major General Weitzel took the White House. Colonel Manning, the Provost Marshal, made his headquarters in the old City Hall and later in the Old Stone House. On that day and for several weeks afterward Richmond women would not show their faces at doors, windows or on the streets.

On April 5th a stranger arrived from Old Point, by steamer, with a party consisting of a few marines and some friends. Accompanied by these President Lincoln rode from the wharf to what had been a few days before the White House of the Confederacy, and partook of a collation there. As he passed through the streets most of the citizens held coldly aloof, though they offered him no disrespect on this his first and last visit to Richmond; but a crowd composed largely of negroes gave him an enthusiastic welcome. After spending several hours in consultation with General Weitzel he passed through the streets to his boat again, and away. Many other Northerners visited the distressed city, for many reasons. Some wished to see for themselves a place which had become so famous. Writers and artists were sent to make sketches for newspapers and magazines. Others hoped to find ways of making money there. Of course interest in the battlefields drew—and still draws—many tourists.

On Sunday, April 9th, a long, miserable week after the message to President Davis in St. Paul's Church, General Lee surrendered to General Grant, at Appomattox. The news brought grief to the people of conquered Richmond, but to the Federal soldiers occupying it, exultation —which they expressed by firing two hundred guns in Capitol Square.

Copyright by W. W, Foster

NEW MAYO'S BRIDGE AND PART OF THE BURNED DISTRICT FIFTY-EIGHT YEA

By courtesy of Richmond Chamber of Commerce

THE BURNED DISTRICT FIFTY-EIGHT YEARS AFTER. FROM TWELFTH STREET, LOOKING WEST
By courtesy of Richmond Chamber of Commerce

CHAPTER XXXV

RECONSTRUCTION

WAR was over. Defeat was acknowledged, but defeat without dishonor. Poverty reigned, but poverty without shame. It was a sign of what Richmond had suffered in a defense of which it was proud. A large proportion of the young manhood on which Richmond set its highest hopes for the future lay dead, but courage was not dead. And without delay Richmond braced itself for the task of rebuilding. On April 11th, President Lincoln raised the blockade of Virginia ports and business communication with the outside world became possible—though no one could leave the city without an order from the President, the Secretary of War, or General Grant.

The apparently conciliatory attitude of President Lincoln when he issued his first amnesty proclamation was harshly criticized by Northern extremists. The call for a meeting of the State Legislature, which filled Virginians with hope was promptly countermanded by the new Federal commander, General Ord. Though war was over, real peace was not yet. The old building with the sign " L. Libby and Son, Ship Chandlers," was still a prison—but it now housed a great number of Confederates. In the burnt district, property owners were seen cleaning bricks, preparatory to rebuilding, and young men of prominent families hired themselves out for this work.

General Ord's reports to the Secretary of War give a grim picture of the Richmond scene, with its thousands of paroled soldiers of General Lee's Army unable to get to their homes, and 26,000 people " of all classes without money or food." He was opening shops where women could be employed by the Quartermaster's Department. A number of well known Confederate Generals and " many prominent and formerly wealthy citizens were asking what they could do to earn their bread." General Ord helped conditions by furnishing transportation home for families who had refugeed in Richmond. A Relief Commission formed to take care of the starving people, divided the city into thirty districts and organized house-to-house visiting. Where need was found, ration tickets were issued which entitled the bearer to pork, or fish, or beef and corn meal, or flour; sugar, and tea. In the seventeen days from the entrance of the Federal army into Richmond, to April 21st, no less than 128,132 rations were issued.

On the second of May, General Dent (who had become Military Governor of Richmond) wrote to his brother-in-law, General Grant: " There is a starving multitude here." Some had money to buy food, but there was no food for sale. Twenty thousand negroes " mostly idle and destitute " were in the town. On June 22d, General Halleck said that they had increased to thirty or thirty-five thousand. They were free, but as yet they did not know what to do with freedom. Many of them thought that it meant freedom to live in idleness and to commit crime.

Even amid such dark scenes as have been pictured there were colorful bits of by-play. On a day soon after Richmond's occupation by the Blue army, a troop of cavalry jogging along Grace Street (doubtless on their way to camp for fresh rations) passed a group of children with their nurses. Some of the cavalrymen hailed " Bub " and " Sis "— titles strange to the ears of Richmond youngsters—and asked if they would like to have some cakes. Though coming from the dreaded Yankees, the prospect of such a treat was welcome, and children and nurses joyfully snatched up the hard, dry sugar-cakes which the soldiers took from their haversacks and tossed to the sidewalk. In the memory of at least one man still living in Richmond, who was one of those fortunate wee rebels, the incident is a bright spot; for it was—so far as he can recall—his earliest acquaintance with cakes.

On what a few years ago was one of the quietest of down-town blocks in Richmond stands a plain, substantial brick house which was in its prime a typical home for a Richmond gentleman of comfortable means, with a family of cheerful size and enough servants to make life easy. This was the war residence of General Lee, and is now the home of the Virginia Historical Society. Of late, tides of business have eaten their way into this quiet cove. Newness and progress press it hard, but it serenely watches the world go by. It was to this home that, on April 15th, General Lee returned from Appomattox. A now venerable lady who from her porch nearby witnessed his return says of it:

" He rode Traveller, and was, as usual a commanding figure, though his grey coat was dingy from hard service, and both he and the horse looked tired and dispirited. His expression, though calm, was unutterably sad. With him came some of his staff, gaunt and pallid, in ragged uniforms, on bony, weary old horses. Dilapidated army wagons creaked after them. One of these was covered with an old quilt in place of the customary canvas. Not a very inspiring cavalcade, it would seem, yet when the blue-coated soldiers of the winning side, who then occupied the city recognized the defeated hero, the air rang with cheers, loud and prolonged. General Lee acknowledged this tribute by gravely lifting his hat. Again and again the cheers rang out. Again and again they were acknowledged in the same manner, until he reached his home. Here he dismounted and still acknowledging the vociferous greetings of the men in blue, backed up the stone steps of his house and through its door, which closed behind him."

Soon after that door had shut General Lee in with his family a friend went to him with the news of President Lincoln's assassination. Deeply shocked, he exclaimed: " This is the hardest blow the South has yet received." Prophetic words, the hardships of the reconstruction was to prove them! Yet, for the present, no one realized how prophetic they were. The new President, Andrew Johnson, seemed inclined to carry out the moderate policies of his predecessor and the conciliatory spirit of Governor Pierpont filled the people with hope, when (with the so-called government of Virginia which had been set up in Alexandria) he was transferred to Richmond. And now soldiers from Northern prisons began to stream into Richmond. Homeless, penniless, hungry, ragged, almost —or quite—barefoot, they came; but still singing the old Southern melodies, fighting battles over again in reminiscent talk, sparkling with quip and jest, whenever two or more of them came together, and laughingly telling one another how they had " worn themselves out whipping Yankees." Numbers of them wore Confederate uniforms —their only clothes. The military guards would cut off the buttons and let them pass; for in the Capital of the Confederacy, Confederate buttons—like Confederate flags —were banned by law. Richmond women did everything they could for the veterans' comfort, and (poor as the people were now that Confederate money was entirely worthless, and they had little else) they held a massmeeting and raised funds to help the soldiers on their way to their families.

And what of the President of the Confederacy? As the murdered Abraham Lincoln was the martyr of the war, the living Jefferson Davis was its scapegoat. President Johnson had offered $100,000 for his capture and Richmond learned with distress that he had been taken prisoner by Federal soldiers, in Georgia, and with his family, the Confederate Vice-President, Postmaster General and others, was confined at Fortress Monroe. The dignity and patience with which he bore the humiliations of his life there and the confiscation of his Mississippi home—"Beauvoir"—and his denial of citizenship in the reunited country, endeared him to the people of Richmond and the South. His home was restored to him in his old age and there he died—but still a man without a country, save one which was only a memory of a four-years-long dream. Its erstwhile Capital—Richmond—received his dead body with profound respect and affection and gave it a statesman's burial in Hollywood—in a spot overlooking the Falls of James River. Members of his family sleep near him—including "Winnie" born at the "White House" and always known as "the Daughter of the Confederacy." An idealized portrait of her may be seen in the marble angel by Zolnay, upon her grave, and her father's monument is a bronze statue of himself.

Though the treatment of the people of Richmond by some of the military officers was (as has been shown) humane, there was intense bitterness in Washington against the "rebels." Under an order of the United States Attorney General, Richmond men who owned any considerable amount of property were forbidden to raise money on it —even for the rebuilding of their city. Later, less discouraging measures were adopted. In the fall of 1865, local judges prepared to open court, but were forbidden to do so by the military authorities. However, in December, met a legislature really representing the people—the last such which was permitted for several years. It planned many things for the welfare of the state and Richmond rejoiced in the belief that the New Year would usher in a brighter era, and that a civil government was about to take the place of a military one. This hope was short-lived. As the year 1866 progressed negroes crowded into the city from the country, and incendiary speeches of Wardwell, Hunnicutt and other Northern " carpet baggers " of their stripe stirred up trouble among the worst elements. The radicals in Congress were bent on a reconstruction of the South which would have placed all intelligence under dominance of ignorance and hatred.

On March 13th, 1867, every semblance of local civil government in Richmond and the state disappeared and military government was given absolute control. Virginia lost even her time-honored and beautiful name and became " District Number One." Fortunately, her first commander, General Schofield, was a fair-minded and generous-hearted man. John C. Underwood, the United States District Judge, seemed to think that his function was to be an instrument of oppression to the conquered Confederates. Such bitter and abusive language had never before disgraced the bench in Virginia and quotation from it shall not besmirch the pages of this chronicle of Virginia's Capital. It was in this man's court that Jefferson Davis was indicted. When the distinguished prisoner was brought into Richmond the people who crowded the streets could only look upon him in silent sympathy. When however, he was granted bail, and Judge Underwood had to say: " The Marshal will discharge the prisoner ", the crowded courtroom and its surroundings rang with cheers which the waiting people in the Square and the streets took up and echoed and re-echoed.

The distress of the people was increased for a time by extravagantly high rents, but as business improved conditions became better. Notwithstanding all difficulties and

216

RECONSTRUCTION

the rigor of military rule the upbuilding of the city continued and by the middle of 1867 eleven banks were open.

Though so intent upon their city's restoration, memories of the "late war" and devotion to those who had fallen in it were ever present, and when Memorial Days came round Richmond flocked to Oakwood and Hollywood to care for and decorate with flowers graves of the men who had died in the Confederate service. When the sun was setting, young surviving comrades of these were seen streaming back into town in a long column, many carrying picks and spades on their shoulders and all singing loved old songs.

On December 3d, 1867, a Constitutional Convention which contained many negroes, carpet-baggers, and scalawags, and was known as the "black and tan" Convention, met in the storied Hall of the House of Delegates. Their Constitution was grudgingly accepted by the people, but a combination of such Virginians as were enfranchised with the better class of Republicans, elected, as "Conservative" governor, Gilbert C. Walker, of New York. He had been a Colonel in the Federal Army, but the people had enough confidence in the fairness of his intentions toward Virginia and her Capital to give him an old time ovation when he arrived in Richmond in July, 1869.

On January 24th, 1870, a welcome sound rang out in Richmond's streets. A sound as cheerful as New Year's bells ringing out the old, ringing in the new. Small black "newsies" with papers under their arms were crying an extra: "All 'bout Virginny back in de Union."

It was true! Congress had passed the bill admitting her. A hundred guns were fired from Capitol Square next day at twelve o'clock, for though many and serious tasks yet lay ahead of Richmond, the long agony of War and Reconstruction was in the past.

EPILOGUE
THE NEW RICHMOND

Now see the remnant of Richmond men who went with a shout to defend their city turn with a will to restore it. Beside them are the women who stoutened their hearts for battle; who strengthen their arms for the rebuilding. And, half a century later, see Richmond after its baptism in blood, in tears and in fire—after a long, long travail, born again into a new city. Its many scars are gone, but reminders that it is a city with a story are scattered through it, not only in such old houses as remain, but in monuments in marble, in stone and in bronze; in the names of streets, of parks, of schools, and of public buildings and institutions. The " Court End " of the city has gone. The modern Juggernaut, Business, is riding relentlessly up homelike Grace and Franklin Streets, but here and there throughout the city quaintness peeps engagingly over the shoulder or under the nose of newness—as where the ancient iron railing still encloses quiet Capitol Square (and its hundreds of unafraid squirrels) from the traffic-filled street above which towers the Reserve Bank. On midsummer days the watermelon vendor, with his small canopied cart, his mule, and his switch with its leaves left on for a combination fly-brush and whip, cries his wares through the long new as he did through the little old streets. Yonder grey-beard, in faded Confederate uniform sunning himself on a green bench, with his crutch beside him, on the green velvet of William Byrd Park is a member of the dwindling family in the Soldiers' Home nearby. The very name of this park conjures up a picture quainter than the veteran—a picture of a figure in the curling locks and gallant dress of the 18th Century, planning the foundation of Richmond and writing in his journal: " Thus did we build not castles only, but cities in the air."

THE FEDERAL RESERVE BANK
Seen from within Capitol Square

THE COUNTRY CLUB OF VIRGINIA, RICHMOND

BROAD STREET STATION

THE NEW RICHMOND

The year 1870, which brought to Richmond the end of the Reconstruction era brought also its share of trouble. The giving way of a floor in an overcrowded courtroom in the Capitol caused many deaths and injuries—when some of the foremost men in the State lost their lives. A widely destructive freshet and the burning of Spotswood Hotel were among the year's sad events. But such disasters had only a temporary effect on a city whose business quarter was being diligently rebuilt, whose business itself was being determinedly revived—often with the aid of Northern Capital. Growth from a population of 51,000 in 1870 to 180,000 in 1922 sometimes slowed down, but never halted. The James River and Kanawha Canal had to be again made navigable, railroads rebuilt, and extended before Richmond could expand satisfactorily. After a while the canal boats, like the old stages, disappeared entirely. They had served their purpose—had their day. Now life was adding to its comforts and losing its picturesqueness. People went travelling in the less leisurely, less sociable railway cars. Through lines north and south, west and southwest were opened; for a time easy rail communication with Virginia seaports made river navigation of less importance than in earlier days, though the river is now coming into its own again and attracting more and more attention from new Richmond business men.

Filling in vacant spots, building up trade, amassing capital, attracting new settlers, Richmond grew and grew and grew. One does not have to be old to remember when the city ended, to the westward, in old fields and small farms at the present site of Stuart Monument and Circle, and when there was an outcry against placing Lee Statue " outside of town, in a mudhole." But this was gradually hushed as wide, tree-lined streets were laid out and homes, churches and schools sprang up around and beyond the " old field " (used as a drillground by the

RICHMOND: ITS PEOPLE AND ITS STORY

Virginia volunteers assembled in Richmond for the war with Spain) where Lee on " Traveller " rides, and stretched away until the inner line of Confederate earthworks, now marked by a cannon mounted on the greensward in the middle of Monument Avenue, was left far behind. Seven miles of electric railway—the first successful trolley line in the world—was Richmond's earliest agent for expansion. Later, automobiles have scattered Richmond families through what would have been hitherto considered distant country localities, until in every direction may be seen houses and gardens of people with business in Richmond who come to town by local train, trolley or automobile. Along the River Road, passing " Tuckahoe ", the old Randolph plantation where Jefferson lived as a child; along with the Three Chopt and Broad Street Roads they lie, and on Brook Road—where formerly the huge canvas-covered wagons whose owners drove them by day and slept in them or put up at some wayside inn or farm house at night, hauled produce from distant counties and mountain regions, and over which stages brought passengers and mail from Northern cities. Southward they are scattered along the Buckingham Road (locally known as the Midlothian Pike), which was the stage route to Lynchburg and over which much tobacco was rolled and coal hauled; and on the Petersburg Turnpike beginning in the old town of Manchester (now part of Richmond), crossing Falling Creek near the site of the first American Iron Works, to the great tobacco growing counties of the Southside. Eastward, north of the river, on the Osborne Road, and the road by which historic " Shirley ", " Berkeley " and " Westover " may be reached; on the Williamsburg Road, the Mechancisville Turnpike, and other roads up and down which moved blue and grey armies in 1861-65, these homes of every description—cottage, bungalow and mansion—bask in peace.

GARDEN AT "LABURNUM", BROOK ROAD
The home of Mr. and Mrs. John Stewart Bryan
By courtesy of Mrs. Bryan

LILAC TIME IN THE GARDEN AT "REVEILLE", CARY STREET ROAD
The home of Mr. and Mrs. E. M. Crutchfield
By courtesy of Mrs. Crutchfield

"PAXTON", CARY STREET ROAD
The home of Mr. and Mrs. John Skelton Williams

IN THE TERRACED GARDEN AT "MAYMONT"
The home of Mrs. James H. Dooley

THE NEW RICHMOND

Suburban parks and country clubs with their playgrounds and swimming pools have given Richmond people new recreational life.

Richmond has had in the past many private schools and teachers of more than local note—teachers whose personality has been a force in the life and character of their pupils. By many Richmond parents of today the precepts of Mr. McGuire, Captain McCabe, Mr. Norwood, Miss Gussie Daniel, Miss Jessie Gordon, Miss Maria Blair, Mr. Powell and others of as ripe scholarship, as pure character, as gentle breeding and as great personal charm are still cherished, and are quoted to boys and girls at the feet of the able successors of those and other school masters and mistresses whose work though laid down is still, subtly, going on. A general system of public schools for white and colored children which began in a crude way immediately after the Reconstruction, has developed and expanded far beyond the dreams of its founders. Institutions for higher education of men and women have progressed in the same degree. The Medical College of Virginia still uses for some of its purposes the unique "haunted" house around which have grown up stories weird enough to have originated in the brain of Poe, but most of the work is done in the more commodious modern building. This College and many hospitals scattered about town make Richmond a centre of medical, surgical and pharmaceutical teaching and a resort of people in and far beyond Virginia, seeking recovery of health. Richmond College (which has removed several miles into the country and expanded into a university with a co-ordinate college for women) now occupies a harmonious group of buildings, in charming grounds, equipped for athletic events.

Northward, Union Theological Seminary (Presbyterian) makes another village-like cluster of buildings—

deep red brick in a setting of deep green foliage. Still another impressive north-side group (in massive grey stone) is that of Virginia Union University, for negro students, with Hartshorn Memorial College—also for negroes—on a pretty campus not far away.

While sociability and fondness for social pleasure is, as it has ever been,'perhaps the leading characteristic of Richmond people, the various circles of its society are still distinguished for culture, and for the large percentage of people identified with them who enjoy intellectual pursuits. Since Richmond people have been able to spare time from the distinctly practical ways of bread-winning which absorbed the population after the War and Reconstruction periods, the city has produced quite a galaxy of authors of national and some of international note, and some artists and musicians to be proud of. If the nature of their work has made it necessary for some of these to become citizens of the world, it has not kept them from continuing to call Richmond " home."

Notable among them was Thomas Nelson Page, who, when a young Richmond lawyer in 1883, waked to find himself famous as the author of " Marse Chan." After a literary career—much of which was spent in Washington—and six years as Ambassador to Italy, he had a few weeks before his death, come home to Virginia and planted a new roof-tree in Richmond. To James Branch Cabell, Richmond is emphatically home though he lives at " Dumbarton Lodge," in a suburb.

Long after the last Confederate has answered the final roll call his appearance in camp and on battlefield will be vividly familiar through the drawings and paintings of William L. Sheppard, the artist who saw service throughout the war in the Richmond Howitzers, and his friend John Elder, who also painted the Confederate soldier from intimate personal knowledge.

THE NEW RICHMOND

Richmond has always been a Sunday-keeping community. New Richmond has many new Churches for white and for colored people, but those which architecturally and historically belong to other days and contribute to suggestions of mellow background, which stimulate memory and imagination, have never been permitted to decay.

Of course New Richmond, like every other city of today, has a growing number of apartment houses equipped with every luxury save the sense of permanency and peace given by long association (sometimes inherited association) and that seclusion which one's very own walls and shrubbery and one's own problems of plumbers and provender impart. And of course there are more and more people who decide that the real way to secure peace is to avoid these very problems. Many of rejuvenated Richmond's newest homes flaunt a fanlight, a brass knocker or white columns—doubtless from a sense of what is becoming in an old and storied city. Inside of them too, are reminders of the past in mantel and cornice, in doorframe or window seat and some of them are rich in heirlooms—in Sheraton tables and Chippendale chairs, in grandmother's cupboards and grandfather's clocks, in portraits in oil by early American painters and portraits in crayon and pastel by St. Memin and Sharples, in Wedgwood and luster, in silver and china. Within some of these too, may still be found a few perfect specimens of a rapidly vanishing type—the genuine old lady. Enthroned in a "wing" chair, beside a wood fire, looking like a twin sister of " Whistler's Mother ", she makes an alluring picture of serenity personified.

" Way down town ", in the Old Market district the ghost of old Richmond walks in broad daylight for the delectation of anyone who will wend his devious way through the cobblestoned streets that lead to it. If he will keep his eyes open he may have a glimpse of an original fanlight—grimy, but graceful—above some battered door, or a finely patterned iron balcony still clinging to a sagging wall. It is in the Old Market that the covered cart with its darky and its mule still flourishes in goodly number, and there women with ebon skins and snow-white, sparkling teeth laugh and chatter or croon old melodies as they shell blackeye peas or make up nosegays that charm coin from the most canny of purses. From gardens of vague regions " somewhere " in the country whence the covered carts have come, they bring, in season, sweet violets and sprays of lilac and bridalwreath which are the spirit of spring made tangible, and wreaths and bunches of holly which create warmth and cheer on the bleakest day hoary winter can show.

Way down town, too, are those unique institutions upon which the fortunes of early Richmond were in great part founded, and many of those of new Richmond still thrive—tobacco factories. These (including the cigar and cigarette factories) today give means of bread-winning to thousands of persons—men and women, old and young, white and colored—and carry the solace of pipe-dreams from Richmond into every town and hamlet in the world. Long before their barnlike walls are sighted a pungent odor with a quality of enchantment peculiar to these factories and their product greets the nostrils. As the visitor draws near enough to hear the chanting of negro " stemmers " he might well wonder if he is not approaching an old plantation, instead of a modern factory. But these are not the only factories in the new-old city. " Way down town ", which in 1865 was an ash-heap, which, even now, is sometimes spoken of as " the burnt district ", business buzzes, traffic roars, sky-scrapers soar to heaven and numberless smokestacks proclaim that everything in the world, from matches to locomotives is made in Richmond.

PLACES OF SPECIAL INTEREST MENTIONED IN THIS VOLUME

PLACES OF SPECIAL INTEREST

PLACES OF SPECIAL INTEREST

AMONG INTERESTING HOMES OVER A CENTURY OLD, SOME OF WHICH ARE NOT MENTIONED IN THIS BOOK, ARE THE FOLLOWING:

Archer House and Garden: Sixth and Franklin Streets.

Brockenbrough House (White House of the Confederacy, now Confederate Museum): Clay and Twelfth Streets.

Caskie House: Fifth and Main Streets.

Coles House (now part of Monte Maria Convent).

"Columbia": Lombardy and Grace Streets.

Craig House (birthplace of Poe's "Helen"): Grace Street, between Eighteenth and Nineteenth Streets.

Jarvis House and Studio: Broad Street, near Monumental Church.

John Marshall House (now headquarters of the Association for the Preservation of Virginia Antiquities): Marshall and Ninth Streets.

McRae House: Ninth and Marshall Streets.

Old Stone House: Main and Nineteenth Streets.

Wickham House and Garden (now Valentine Museum, filled with objects of interest, including large collection of Indian relics): Clay and Eleventh Streets.

Woodbridge House: Grace and Seventh Streets.

Many modern houses bear tablets marking historic sites—as that on Main and Third Streets, showing the location of the Sally Tompkins Hospital.

In Hollywood, memorials of a host of notables besides those named (including John Randolph and General Stuart) attract the pilgrim, while in the earlier Shockoe Hills Cemetery lie hundreds of the makers of *old* Richmond. There, Chief Justice Marshall and his friend, Parson Blair, are neighbours, and near them sleeps "Poe's Helen," with a stanza celebrating his devotion, on a bronze tablet at the base of her monument. Poe's mother rests under the sod of St. John's churchyard, which is filled with mossy marbles bearing quaint epigraphs. A group composed largely of Alumni of the University and members of the theatrical profession are about to place a stone over her grave.

INDEX

A

"Abbington," 20
Academy, The, 56–59, 61; Square, 57, 69, 104
Adams, President, 89; John, 121, Richard, 21, 36; Street, 21
African Church, First, 125, 157, 158, 161
Agricultural Fair, 157
Alabama Hospital, 182
Albemarle County, 21
Alexandria, Va., 107, 183
Allan, John, 104, 107, 135, 136; House, 100
Allegrè, Miss, 96
Ambler, Jacqueline, 89, 93; John, 93; Polly, 89 et seq.
American Iron Works, First, 220
"Ampthill," 24, 39
Amusements and Entertainments, 22, 45, 49, 53, 55, 56, 74, 75, 91–94, 97, 120–123, 138, 139
Anburey's Travels, 39
Anderson's Tavern, 50, 55
Appomattox, 210, 213
Archer, Gabriel, XVIII, 4, 5
"Arlington," 166
Armory, The, 75, 83, 171
Arnold, Benedict, 39 et seq.
Ashland, 189, 196, 197
Association for the Preservation of Virginia Antiquities, 13, 54, Illustration, 55
Athenaeum, The, 130, 138, 140
Atkinson, Nicholas, 55
Austin, Capt. John, 54
Aylett, William, 36

B

Bacon, Elizabeth, 12; Nathaniel, 12, 13, 24; Thomas, 12; —'s Quarter, 12, 74; —'s Rebellion; 12, 13
Bagby, George, 137
Baker, Jack, 95, 98
Ballard House, 156, 190, 199
Banister, John, 18

Bank Street, 78
Bank of Virginia, 95, 128; of Richmond, 78
Banks, Linn, 118
Banks, 50
Baptist Church, First, 72, 153; Second, Illustration, 168; Church, 72; General Association of Virginia, 153; Woman's College, 93
Barbecue Club, 74
Barbour, James, 109; Philip P., 126
Barret, John, 52
"Battle Abbey" (Illustrations), 199
Baxter, Mrs., 138; Sydney S., 144
Beaver Dam Creek, 190
Beauregard, P., 97, 174
"Beauvoir," 215
Bee, General, 174
"Belinda," 31
Bell Tavern, 49
Bell Tower, 67, 165, 110, Illustration, 71
Belle Isle, 192; Iron Works, 171
Belles, Beaux, and Brains of the Sixties, 176
"Belvidere," 39
Benge, 54
Benjamin, J. P., 187
Bently, 54
Berkeley, Sir William, 10, 12
"Berkeley," 61, 143
Beth Ahabah Synagogue (Illustration), 176
Bethel Church, Battle of, 173, 174
Beveridge, Senator, 61
Beverley, Robert, 15; William, 16
Binkheim, Meyer, 54
Bird, Spottswood, 207
Blagrove, 73
Blair, John D., 72, 74 et seq., 81 111, 120; Maria, 221
Bland, Richard, 30
"Blandfield," 16
Blennerhassett, Herman, 98, 99

229

INDEX

INDEX

INDEX

INDEX

Harrison, Benjamin, 25, 30, 60; William H., 143
Hartshorn College, 122
Harvie, Gabriella, 95; Jacqueline B., 93, 95; John, 95
Hay, George, 95, 96, 97, 98; Mrs. George, 97; William, 45
Hayes - Green - McCance House, 96, and Illustration
Haymarket Garden, 103; Stables, 55
Henrico County, 7, 9, 21, 23
Henry, 57; John and Joseph, 52; Patrick, 13, 30, 32, 33, 34, 38, 49, 59, 61, 62, 80
Hill, Ambrose P., 176, 189; D. H., 189; Edward, 8
Hoffbauer (See Illustration), 199
Hoge, Moses D., 184
Hogg's Tavern, 37
Hollingsworth, 52
Hollywood Cemetery, 149, 157, 174, 215
Hooker, Joseph, 197, 198
Hopkins, Mrs. Arthur F., 182
Horsmanden, Warham, 10, 14
Hospital, Sally Tompkins, 182
Houdon, 65, 66, 67, 209
Howard's Grove, 171
Howlett's, 12
Humphreys, John, 53
Hunnicutt, 216
Hunt, Gilbert, 105

I

Indian Trading, 10, 11
Indians, 5, 13, 14, 16, 18
Independent Gazetteer, 59
"Inglesby," 20
Inman, Artist, 54, Illustration
Innes, James, 61
Iron Works, First in America, 7
Irving, Washington, 99
Isaacs, 54
Israel, Levi, 54
Ives, Mrs. 187

J

Jackson, Andrew, 112; T. J. (Stonewall), 68, 174, 188, 195, 197, 198; Statue of, 68

James River and Kanawha Canal, 128, 219; James River Canal, 78
Jamestown, 3, 4, 7, 10, 15, 24
Janney, John, 162, 667
Jefferson, Joseph, XX, 141, 142, 157; Illustration, 101; Thomas, 24, 25, 30, 31, 33, 37, 38, 61, 65, 67, 75, 78, 80, 81, 89, 90, 99, 102, 135, 220; Street, 21
Jews, 223
Jockey Club, 91, 122
Johns, John, 175
Johnson, Andrew, 214, 215; Chapman, 94, 126, 127; Edward, 187; Marmaduke, 167; Mrs. Ralph C. (Mattie Waller), 193; William R., 122
Johnston, Mary, 167; Joseph E., 174, 179, 180, 182
Jones, Peter, 18
Jordan's Point, 12
Joseph Bryan Park (Illustration), 191

K

Kennedy, John P., 135
Kent, Paine and Co., 191
Kilpatrick, General, 199
King and Queen County, 200

L

"Laburnum" Garden, Illustration, 208
"Lady Lightfoot" (horse), 122
Lafayette, 41, 42, 43, 49, 107, 117 *et seq;* George Washington, 119
Ladies' Defence Association, 178
Lamar, 187
Lancaster, R. A. Jr., Illustration, 155
"Lancasterian School," 113
Latané, William, 118, 192; Burial of, 192, 193, (Illustraiton), 118
Latrobe, B. H., 78, (Illustration), 27
Lee, Edmond J., 107; Henry, 61; R. H., 30; Robert E., XX, 66, 154, 166 *et seq.*, 180, 181, 185, 188, 189, 191, 192, 195, 198, 199, 201, 202, 205, 206, 210, 211,

233

INDEX

INDEX

INDEX

INDEX

Tompkins, Sally, 182, 183
Totopotomoi, 8
"Traveller" (horse), 202
Tredegar Iron Works, 171, 178
Tree Hill Farm, 208; Race Track, 122
Trigg, William R., 147
"Tuckahoe," 25, 38, 39, 40, 220
Tucker, George, 130
Turnbull, Charles, 24
Turner, Nat, Insurrection, 130, 131
Two Parsons, The, 74
Tyler, John, I, 61, 103; II, 143 *et seq;* 149, 161, 175; President, tomb of (Illustration), 94

U

"Uncle Henry" (Illustration), 77
Underwood, John C., 216
Union Hotel, 120; University, 122
University of Richmond, 221; of Virginia, 136
Union Theological Seminary, 221

V

Valentine, Edward V., 86, 141, 100 (Illustration), 101; Frances, 104; Mann S., 94, 123; William, 86; Museum, 94, 96, 123; Studio, 141
Van Lew, Elizabeth, 200
Venable, Abram B., 105
Virginia (ship), 178
Virginia Bible Society, 110; Colonization Society, 131; *Gazette*, VII, 22, 34, 39, 50; Historical Society, VII, 130, (Illustration), 117, 213; Military Institute, 122, 167; State Library, VII
"Virginian" (horse), 122
Voltaire, 71

W

Waddell, William, 50
Walker, Gilbert C., 217; Hugh, 35
Ward, Maria, 95
Warden, John, 96
Wardwell, 216

Warrenton, James, 52
Warwick, 113; Imogen, 193; House (Illustration), 154
Washington, Bushrod, 107; George, XX, 30, 31, 33, 35, 41, 43, 49, 53, 58, 61, 80, 81, 112, 119–122, 159; Monument (Illustration), 18, 66, 67, 68 175; Statue by Houdon (Illustration), 37; Martha, 168; William D., 109, 193; Tavern, 99
Water Supply, 133
Wayne, Anthony, 42, 43, 119
Webb, Mrs. Lucy Mason, 182
Weisiger, Daniel, 20
Weitzel, General, 208, 210
Wellford, Spotswood, 183
West, Francis, 7
West Fort, 7
West and Johnston, 198
Westham Foundry, 40, 43, 44
Westhampton College (women), 221
Westmorland Club, 138 (Illustration), 155, 187
"Westover," 15, 17, 41, 191
"Westwood," 192, 193
Whigparty, 143 *et seq;* 155
White, T. W., 136; William H., 173; William S., 162
White House of Confederacy, 95, 108, 109, 169, 176, 177, 215, (Illustration), 108
Wickham, John (portrait), 62, 96, 98, 100; Mrs. John (portrait) 62; Julia, 94
Wilderness, Battle of, 201
William Byrd Park, 218
William Byrd Park, Boulevard Approaching (Illustration), 191
William and Mary College, 38, 81, 89
Williamsburg, 24, 29, 34, 37, 39, 59; Road, 180, 220
Williams, Mr. and Mrs. John Skelton, Home of (Illustration), 207
Wilson, Thomas, 112
"Wilton," 24, 38
Wirt, William, 95, 96, 98, 100, 111
Wise, Henry A., 154

INDEX